Fascist Mythologies

NEW DIRECTIONS IN CRITICAL THEORY

NEW DIRECTIONS IN CRITICAL THEORY
Amy Allen, General Editor

New Directions in Critical Theory presents outstanding classic and contemporary texts in the tradition of critical social theory, broadly construed. The series aims to renew and advance the program of critical social theory, with a particular focus on theorizing contemporary struggles around gender, race, sexuality, class, and globalization and their complex interconnections.

For a complete list of titles, see page 171

Fascist Mythologies

THE HISTORY AND POLITICS
OF UNREASON IN BORGES,
FREUD, AND SCHMITT

Federico Finchelstein

Columbia University Press

New York

Columbia University Press
Publishers Since 1893
New York   Chichester, West Sussex
cup.columbia.edu

Library of Congress Cataloging-in-Publication Data
Names: Finchelstein, Federico, 1975– author.
Title: Fascist mythologies : the history and politics of unreason in Borges,
Freud, and Schmitt / by Federico Finchelstein.
Description: New York : Columbia University Press, [2022] |
Includes bibliographical references and index.
Identifiers: LCCN 2021036400 (print) | LCCN 2021036401 (ebook) |
ISBN 9780231183208 (hardback) | ISBN 9780231183215 (trade paperback) |
ISBN 9780231544795 (ebook)
Subjects: LCSH: Fascism. | Myth—Political aspects.
Classification: LCC JC481 .F5179 2022 (print) | LCC JC481 (ebook) |
DDC 320.53/3—dc23/eng/20211202
LC record available at https://lccn.loc.gov/2021036400
LC ebook record available at https://lccn.loc.gov/2021036401

Cover design: Noah Arlow
Cover image: Dreamstime

Contents

Preface

MYTH WAS EVERYTHING to the fascists. Fascists stressed how myth was the key to explain the world and, most importantly, their motivation to change it. For Mussolini fascism created its own myth. Myth was "a faith and a passion." Even if at first myths were not part of reality, fascism would turn them into a "complete reality."[1] In fascism, myth imposed itself on reality and therefore reality could not represent an obstacle to myth. The mythical nature of fascism was equally defined by the imposition of peculiar boundaries between fascist truths and the fake nature of the enemy.[2]

Fascists stressed the mythical dimensions of power. They believed that the myths of their leader embodied and carried over previous myths of civilization, the nation, and the people. And yet, the myth or, rather, the myths of fascism belong to the long history of the modern political imagination. These myths are and were related to previous classical myths, but at the same time they were starkly different from them. Fascists pushed political mythology to a political edge never witnessed before in history, fabricating myths to an extent never seen before.

In my work I have addressed these mythical dimensions of fascism. I have studied its different contextual and ideological variations in the development of fascist myth in politics across the Atlantic, especially the years of the age of fascism, between 1919 and 1945.

Adopting a more specific antifascist angle, this book delineates the national and transnational paths that led thinkers like Sigmund Freud and Jorge Luis Borges, who lived and wrote during the processes of ideological construction and practical execution of the myths of fascism, to ponder the conceptual and practical relations between the victims of trauma and the ideological myths of their perpetrators. In other words, in this book I propose that Freud's and Borges's oeuvres can be approached so as to consider the most radical ideological and mythical dimensions of fascism and the Holocaust. I also analyze the key work of the German Nazi thinker Carl Schmitt, who contributed a long, if generally neglected, chapter of this history of the myths of fascism.

Thus, complementing and expanding on my previous works on fascism, dictatorship, and the ideological lies they engender, I emphasize the interpretative perspectives of Freud and Borges and other critical thinkers in relation to the processes of victimization driven by the fundamental mythologies of fascist politics. More specifically, I stress the need to consider these processes as part of a broader spectrum of mythical and traumatic encounters. In these encounters, the sacrifice of the body—either in the form of self-sacrifice or as a direct sacrificial action toward the Other—obeys the mandates of a radical mythical ideology. This ideological situation represented a marked displacement from the classical myth of the hero to the modern mythification of the leader. For this ideology, there were no distinctions between myth, power, and violence.

Fascism is a philosophy of political action that ascribes an absolute political and mythical value to violence and war in the political realm. It conceives of the political field as rooted in primordial instincts and violence. In other words, in fascism the legitimacy of myths is the basis of politics. Violence in its purest form is presented as the foundation of political power. Fascism conceives it as the actualization of a sort of mythical unconscious that lives in man, and that moves throughout history but also transcends it. In this context, the mythology of an inner I, at the same time essentially violent and political, replaces history as the legitimation of action. Fascists believed that true politics was based on the modernization of myth. In a fascist key, this modernization represented a notable actualization of the classical myths. As we will see, this political secularization of the classical heroic myth constituted the myth of fascism.[3]

Fascists of diverse origins and trajectories, from the Italian dictator Benito Mussolini to the Argentine Leopoldo Lugones, shared this perception of the mythical as a new form of politics. They saw it as modern renewal of mass politics, legitimizing an extreme form of authoritarian rule where popular sovereignty was conflated with classical images of the mythological hero as well as with dictatorship as the ultimate expression of the people, the leader, and the nation.

This ideology of myth distills from the infinity of fascist sources across the Atlantic and beyond. For them, the mythical becomes the subject of adoration but also a key source of political legitimacy and mobilization. If, for fascists like Carl Schmitt, this mythical conception cannot be unpacked because it represents a sacred whole, it is the incipient gaze of critical antifascists thinkers in the 1920s and 1930s that reconstitutes the mythology of fascism: from myth to concept, from subject of faith to object of analysis.

Sigmund Freud was one of the first interpreters to explore the mythical dimensions of fascism. He saw it as a mythical reformulation of death and violence that presented them as directly linked to the unconscious. Fascism rejected the Freudian call for building self-reflective bridges between the conscious and the unconscious. Fascist ideology actually put forward the idea that, somehow through a direct connection with the inner self, death and primordial violence would become sources of political power. Freud and also Borges were especially insightful in noticing and analyzing this key dimension of fascism. The book is especially focused on both authors' interpretations of the ideologies and theories of the inner self that fascism read through a mythical prism and why and how that made possible the emergence of fascist genocidal violence.

These discussions often present a history of parallel affinities that as in the cases of Borges and Freud (or even Schmitt) do not present explicit links with each other. However, in many other cases these discussions converge and the actors read and debated each other across the political spectrum. In particular, throughout the interwar and war years, many significant fascists and antifascists read Freud to think, use, or deny his theories about norms, politics, and the unconscious. They did so in a transatlantic context that included antifascists like José Carlos Mariátegui and Ernst Cassirer and fascist ideologues from the Brazilian fascist leader Plinio Salgado to Mussolini and many others.[4] Despite absolute political differences, more precisely defined by the anti-Enlightenment meaning of fascism, many fascists and antifascists stressed the deep relations between fascism, political myth, and leadership. From different positions they all stressed the fascist desire to embrace the power of myths. Or to put it differently, they all stressed that fascists regarded mythical assertions as being more significant than empirical demonstrations.

For antifascists such as Borges and Freud, of course, it was critical that one could not accept the ahistorical premises of fascist mythologies. Fascism demonstrated that the world changed rapidly, from secularism and reason to faith. This was not a mere return of old myths that, in fact, had served a different function. Modern fascist myths promoted dehumanization, obedience, and the rejection of pluralism and autonomy in politics and history. Classical myths or religion no longer played a role in sustaining ethical positions or norms. In this sense Hannah Arendt observed in 1951 that "Whether we like it or not, we have long ceased to live in a world in which the faith in the Judaeo-Christian myth of creation is secure enough to constitute a basis and source of authority for actual laws." For Arendt, the mythical understandings of history "have one characteristic in common: they assume that something was there, given, already established before human history actually began; that, in other words, the direction of history was beyond human effort, that its laws sprang from a transcendent source (or event) and could only be obeyed or disobeyed." This was for Arendt a key dimension behind the crimes of the "tragedy of our time."[5]

For thinkers like Arendt, the mythical breaking-down of reason was an act of self-deception. But Arendt did not sufficiently address why and how myth worked in the first place. In this context, it is especially in the cases of Borges and Freud where we can see a major attempt to think the mythical from within, without subscribing to its transcendental assumptions, fantasies, and imaginary elements. In contrast, the mythological thinking of Carl Schmitt presented a complex illustration of thinking the mythical while rejecting reason. As I will show, the result of this attempt was a critical consideration regarding the limits and reach of the dichotomy between myth and reason and how the emphasis in this dichotomy was central to the ideology of fascism. In our own present, where myth and political lies have returned to the center of politics, the antifascist critiques of Borges and Freud acquire a new force. Their critique of the myth of fascism provides us with tools to fight the new dangerous mythologies of the present.

Fascist Mythologies

{ 1 }

Myth and Fascism

WITH THE BIRTH OF FASCISM, myth became one and the same with propaganda. Demonstration was replaced with fabrication. The sacred took the place of the secular. Extraordinary explanation eliminated common sense. By the end of the Second World War, the antifascist German Jewish thinker Ernst Cassirer arrived at these conclusions after an academic life dedicated to the study of mythical configurations. Modern propaganda was, above all, mythmaking. He wrote that myth was not only far removed from empirical reality, but it was, "in a sense, in flagrant contradiction to it." Logically this would mean that most people could find myth a thing hard to believe in. In other words, myths were figments of the imagination and could not explain reality. But the opposite was true. As Cassirer observed, lots of people believed in mythical things that did not exist. Irrational believers especially were those who trusted fascist lies and propaganda. Cassirer, like the Argentine writer Jorge Luis Borges before him, was not alone in thinking myth as key component of fascism.

For Borges, in fascism history was reduced to myth, and the past became "a mythology of hate." A few months after the Nazi rise to power in 1933, the Argentine intellectual warned that if a world war was to "explode on Monday by Tuesday this planet will be swimming in [a sea] of mythologies." For Borges, the appeal of myth as a "false memory" of the past could be explained by the fact that "lies" offered simple and understandable explanations. History, in contrast, was messy and full of "confusing horrors." He denounced mythical binary thinking as presenting two sides, "light" and "perdition." This had been the case with the Great War and also with the Argentine dictatorship of 1930.[1] In fact, like many other antifascists, Borges did not distinguish between myth and propaganda, but like Cassirer he pointed out how in fascism the outcome of myth was extreme violence and even a will to die for the leader. What kind of people could choose death over life?

Writing in 1944, Theodor Adorno explained that the "paranoid mind" paid a big price for its absolute judgments. The price was ignoring reality, or, as he put it, losing the experience of the matter that was under consideration. Adorno also defined irrationalism as the postulation of "arbitrary theses justified by an intuitive faith in revelation."[2] This was at the center of the cult of the leader. A relapse into sacralizing thinking made followers rely on the leader's untruth and the result was total blindness.[3] The word of fascism became the single answer to the riddles of the universe. This is why for Hannah Arendt Nazism was so highly ideological.[4]

Nearing the end of his life, Cassirer wondered why myth was so predominant in politics: "The preponderance of mythical thought over rational thought in some of our modern political systems is obvious. After a short and violent struggle mythical thought seemed to win a clear and definitive victory. How was this victory possible?" Part of his answer was the surrendering of rational logic to the faith in leaders that promised to bring back a golden past. This prophetic conductor personified an "inevitable, inexorable, irrevocable destiny," and yet despite the actual historical connections between leaders like Adolf Hitler and the mythical traditions of the past, Cassirer concluded that, unlike classical myths, modern political myths were not societal beliefs but contemporary fabrications of fascist propaganda men.[5]

Cassirer's distinction between old and new myths remains of key importance. But both still share key features. In its classic form, myth can be better understood as a "fictitious" collective narrative that was widely accepted and was felt as real although it was situated outside of history and featured characters of divine or heroic nature. Both classical and modern myths present their narrative of the primordial origins of the world as the ultimate explanation for the mystery of human existence, which in turn provides a direct and simple answer to the problems and anxieties of the present.[6] The idea that a sacred, transcendental discourse can reduce all contexts to a single explanation is central to myth and this is why, as Borges suggested, myth is essentially opposed to the modern idea of history. Myth acts as a code to read the connections between past and present, but it lacks any interest in the past as such.

In mythical thinking, as the French historian Jean-Pierre Vernant suggests, the past is seen as a dimension of the beyond: "The past thus revealed is much more than the antecedent of the present; it is its source."[7] As Vernant argues, myth was never static, and in fact, in the classical world there was a semantic evolution of the term *mythos* but it still represented a tale and always stood in dual opposition to the order of the real and argumentative demonstration. For Vernant, mythos simply refers to that which belongs to the order of pure fiction, "the fable." In classic myths the narrative dimension was "quite free" in the sense that there could be multiple and even, at times, contradicting narratives about the sacred or an epic story and they all could coexist "without scandal." Vernant stresses this narrative dimension of the classical myths and how it is historically related to present time phenomena. Myth is connected to "what we call religion and what for us is literature."[8]

3

If the Greeks (or the Aztecs or the Mayans) often created separations between daily experience and mythical explanations, this situation changes with the advent of fascist modernity.[9] In fascism the fabled nature of the myth is converted to the order of the real. Suddenly there are no major distinctions between these two spheres of experience and belief. Myth becomes a principal foundation of political authenticity but also of everyday politics and, more importantly, of the logic of fascism in which you always follow and trust your leader. If classical myths implied a personal removal from the politics of the present, fascist myth provides its ultimate explanation and it does beyond or above empirical demonstration.

For fascists, power and violence are essentially present in the mythical as they incarnate its aspirations and assumptions. They represent the dynamism of life, a life that is authentic and effervescent. In the view of fascism, mythology stands in opposition to a decadent form of reason. In fascism, all that is based on intuition represents authenticity. All that is politically legitimate has roots in collective desires and is not mediated by reason. This ideological stress on the sovereignty of the unconscious delineates a stark difference between fascism and psychoanalysis. In fascist theory, reason plays no role of mediation in the exteriorization of the unconscious. While in psychoanalysis there is no true outing of the unconscious, in fascism its externalization is conceived in mythical terms. In fascism, mythos returns and becomes the mediator between the unconscious and politics.

The relationship between the inner self, mythology, and fascism is part of a larger context in which Freud's original analysis of the mythical and thus unconscious dimension of fascism became a key source for the critical theories of fascist ideology that took place especially in Latin America and Europe.

This line of argument is central in the psychoanalytically inflected works of a variety of transatlantic critical thinkers, from the Frankfurt school, especially in *The Dialectic of the*

Enlightenment (1944), to a varied group of intellectuals on both sides of the Atlantic, for example, Cassirer, José Carlos Mariáte-gui, and Norbert Elias, among many others. These critics elaborated on the emancipatory potential of the psychoanalytic critique of fascism. The rise of fascism highly influenced psychoanalysis. It reshaped previous psychoanalytic understandings of the dangers of mass politics and their global nature. In turn, the Freudian reading of fascism affected interpreters of fascism such as Antonio Gramsci and especially Jorge Luis Borges, who were not explicitly engaged with, and were, at times, even critical of, psychoanalysis.

Thinkers like Gramsci and Borges in fact often assumed toward Freudian theories a stark critical position, but they all shared with Freud the view of the fascist attempt to dilute distinctions between the historical past and the present. They were all concerned about the political implications of the fascist's replacement of the historical past with the mythical past. And they all agreed that in this radical operation, argumentation ceded its place to transcendental postulates that fabricated the mythical to authenticate the political. From an enlightened normative position, thinkers like Borges stressed the key role that political fantasies played in fascism. These fantasies explained the meaning of the universe through their insistence on the unitary identification between myth, ideology, and violence. But if, in Borges, this defense of enlightened norms was shaped as a response to his perception of a barbaric threat to democratic culture, for Freud this defense of the legacy of enlightenment became more introspective.

All in all, Borgean thinking on fascism and the Holocaust reaches a situation of analytical immediacy with Freudian psychoanalysis and its hypothesis regarding the mythical dimensions of fascism as a modern transposition of barbarism and mythology.

In both authors (Borges and Freud) mythology and barbarism are intimately tied. But in Borges, more than in Freud, the intellectual genealogy of the anti-Enlightenment is especially central to explaining fascism. Borges sees the myth of fascism as the symptom of the return of what Enlightenment thinking had overcome. But he also frames the reoccurrence of myth in and through fascism in a broader spectrum: the return to the political myth of the hero as a result of the rejection of secular thought.

For Borges, the rejection of the Enlightenment implies the beginning of fascism. Without a perhaps needed emphasis on other epochal changes such as the First World War, the extended threats and fears of revolution, or the democratic crisis of representation of the interwar period, Borges emphasizes the long-term conceptual origins of fascism. More specifically, in his prologue to Thomas Carlyle's *Heroes* (1949), Borges reduces Carlyle's book to be a prolegomenon of fascism.

This reduction gave Borges an original perspective on the ideology of political myth in fascism while also leading him to miss the interwar context that greatly shaped fascism. Of course, that context also includes the reactionary critique of the democratic legacy of Enlightenment, a critique that goes beyond Carlyle in denouncing reason as a way of thinking about the world and politics.

This Borgesian critique of myth presents it as part and parcel of a political theology. While suggesting that the irruption of antirationalism opens the conceptual doors to the idealization of political myth, Borges presents different contexts of the political conception of the mythical. This critique of the place of rationalism in politics is part of the genealogy of the modern political myth in general and of the mythologies of fascism in particular.

Myth Versus Reason

The critique of the Enlightenment, as the historian Zeev Sternhell has pointed out, is centered on the rejection of universalism and equality. Its intellectual roots are found in thinkers like Giambattista Vico (1688–1744) and above all Johann Gottfried Herder (1744–1803) and Edmund Burke (1722–1797). This critique has three immutable pillars: antirationalism, relativism, and nationalist communitarianism.[10] This reaction prefigures the place of myth in fascist political thinking and occurs first in a broad framework of criticism of the legacy of Enlightenment. It disputes the enlightened rejection of particularism and unverifiable beliefs, as well as its secularism and reason, which formed the foundation of modern politics. This critique also includes thinkers such as Juan Donoso Cortés (1809–1853) and Thomas Carlyle (1795–1881), among many others, who established a framework of reactionary thinking for what they saw as the evil trinity of parliamentarism, liberal democracy, and rationalism. For Donoso, for example, parliamentarism denies government, and liberalism implies the negation of truth and rationalism and is "the affirmation of madness." The Donosian attempt to rethink modern politics is aimed at separating reason from a strictly rationalist framework that humanizes and secularizes it. Donoso presents a new political theology for which revolutions and tyrannies are driven not only by human agency but also by divine sovereignty. It is only God that can place the political domain in the path to true political freedom. This freedom, for Donoso, is Catholic freedom. In this antirationalist framework, what is eminently transhistorical and sacred becomes a source of political sovereignty. Donoso locates sovereignty at the domain of the faith of the people and rejects the sovereignty of secular reason. According to Donoso, it is central in politics to believe in what one can understand but not outside the framework of one's own political theology. Somehow suggesting a fake theology, Donoso denounces the impossibly "supernatural" elements of socialist humanism.[11] He does not speak of political myth, but he put forward an idea of politics that is situated both inside and outside of history. The Spanish thinker adopts the terminology of the

classical myth to accuse his liberal, anarchist, and socialist enemies, whom he places in a clearly historical and not transcendental framework, which to him is a proof their secular untruth.[12]

In Donoso and Carlyle, myth and mythology are not yet part
of new political religions for rethinking politics. In organically
questioning the capabilities and goals of democratic ideas, both
authors, and especially Carlyle, tend to recognize the impossibility of returning to premodern notions of sovereignty. They are
not simple reactionary thinkers. Mythical heroes have a role to
play in their attempt to move modernity in a new authoritarian
direction. This role is no longer an ahistorical escapism from reality, as was the case with classical myths, but rather it is emblem-
atic of a new role for the sacred in modern politics.

For Donoso, human leaders and heroes cannot be absolutely
deified, that is, they should not be fully portrayed as emanations
of the divine. In contrast Carlyle thought this incarnation was
needed and possible. While, for Donoso, this tendency to take
political possession of the divine is in and of itself a product of
socialist rationalism, for Carlyle repossessing the divine represents the possibility of freeing oneself of reason to think modern
politics.[13] Above all, for Carlyle, modern politics must be sacral-
ized and dedemocratized by way of discovering a new charismatic
"Hercules." The role of these modern mythical leaders, storm captains with "command words," is not related to the old aristoc-
racy precisely because it takes up classic models of heroes like
Prometheus.

For Carlyle, although the valuation of the mythical hero in history leads to a modern politicization of the classical myth (Prometheus, Ephimeteus, and Hercules, for example), the word myth
is opposed to knowledge.[14] But after Carlyle and with the widen-
ing of transatlantic democracy, the question of myth as a way of
understanding the mobilization and experiences of collective
subjects tends to displace Carlyle's concern for the hero as the
only mythical key to understanding history and politics. For

example, in thinkers such as Georges Sorel (1847–1922) and later Carl Schmitt (1888–1985), myth becomes a symbol of the revolution, the revolutionary strike, or even politics as such. Myth is the promise of an epochal change. The myth of the hero of classical mythology loses its solitary character to become the pillar of a new historical structure.[15] In Sorel and then in Schmitt, the myth functions as a metaphor for understanding political needs and macrohistorical changes.

For Schmitt, the Christian martyr, the fallen intellectual, or Hamlet himself are symptoms and models of action for understanding history. In contrast, for most fascists, there is no difference between myth and history. Myth is no longer a metaphor but a reality. Myth becomes more than the symptom of something else. With fascism, the myth of the classical hero whose violence is pure resurfaces to become the political program of the leader. He presents himself as a mythical hero. The fascist myth is not part of history as a past but part of the totalitarian politics of the present. For Mussolini, the past, the present, and the future are united in and through political myth. As Mussolini would argue in his famous Naples speech in 1922, fascism represented the creation as well as the resurrection of myth.[16]

This speech represented, for Carl Schmitt, the Sorelian influence in Mussolini; but unlike in Sorel and even Schmitt, the Mussolinian construction of the myth reformulates it as a transcendental reality that is reborn. It is not a mere mobilizing function for politics but the harbinger of totalitarian salvation. Schmitt noted the irrational dangers that the political myth augured but defined them as abstract and therefore less important than the new reality that was represented by the political myth of fascism and that could not be ignored. For Schmitt, "the modern theory of myth" was "the most powerful symptom" of the decline of liberalism.[17] For Mussolini, the myth was not only a denunciation of the democratic present; it also implied the theological certainty of a future.

As the antifascist Piero Gobetti noted at the time, for Mussolini there was no difference between myths and history.[18] However, Mussolini never attempted to reflect on what he saw as a natural combination of mythical and historical forces. For the Duce, socialism was a "lower mythology" because it was not mythical enough. For him, there was no danger in irrationalism and in its promise of war and violence. For fascism, the reality of mythology, and its ideal of violence in its original state, displaced the rational reality of the present, transcended the mythical construction itself, and represented the ideological truth that would be imposed on reality.

For fascists, myth is a reality that transcends the verifiable and the earthly. In fascism, the myth of the hero is confused with a new trinity: leader, nation, people. To put it another way, in the political religion of fascism, incarnation merges with two concepts. One is territorial (the nation) and another is a collective subject (the people). The fascists go beyond Sorel and Schmitt by incorporating their functionalist perception of the myth as a way to strategically mobilize the masses into an absolute belief in the myth based on faith.

For fascism, with the return of myth, man must abdicate reason in order to believe. This stripping of reason would create the new man. Borges saw this central dimension of fascism, but he explained it by going back to Carlyle's thought. For Borges, Carlyle is less an ideological influence than a symptomatic premonition of the mythology of fascism, in particular his attempt to present a "theory of history" in which the modern myths of the heroes act as classical myths. This idea of the totalitarian translation of the mythical is central to the Argentine writer's critique of fascism.

Borges criticizes the fascist idea of the past according to which the narrative is articulated from the divine mission of the hero. The Argentine writer suspects the political myths of the hero, and his results "rushed to the dregs" by Italy, Germany, and Russia:

the "abolition of parliaments and the unconditional surrender of power to strong and silent men." The totalitarian dictatorship eliminates context, turns history into mythology, and promotes "servility, fear, brutality, mental destitution and denunciation."[19]

This totalitarian regression of history into mythology breaks the distinctions between mythos and logos. This unification of logos and mythos only allows for a "theory of history" and not history itself. The result of the lack of context in thought is the unleashing of barbaric violence. In Borges, as well as in other critical interpreters of fascist mythologies, the return of violence implies an abysmal break in normativity. Mythical violence is outside the law because it is against all laws.

Freudian psychoanalysis also had a normative, and even moralistic, theory of the unconscious, that is, the idea that desire (the id) is potentially negative and should be repressed, controlled, and eventually confronted through language and the law. In short, it has to be articulated in rational terms but not necessarily in historical ones. For Freud, language, rather than images, inarticulate feelings, or actions, represented the only form of elaboration. The articulation of words provided the only rational approach to the depths of the unconscious. Other intellectuals, particularly those attracted to fascism, did not agree. Georges Bataille, for example, preferred to emphasize the power of fascism's attachment to the inner self of the ego, or what Freud called the unconscious. Bataille arguably became something close to a fellow traveler of fascism, and his fascination with its ideology is related to what he perceived as the fascist emphasis on homogenous inner structures.[20] For well-known Italian fascists like Mussolini and Curzio Malaparte or Argentines and Brazilians such as Leopoldo Lugones and Plinio Salgado, fascism represented bare power. They saw fascism as a political formation largely driven, and constantly regenerated, by its inner "sacred" will. For them, fascism is a political structure whose special engine and agent of continuous regeneration were myths. For all of them, the sacrality of the I had to be reasserted in the mythical apparatus of fascism as the expression of the authentic inner self. This self was for fascism a transhistorical expression of the nation, which, in turn, they understood as transcendental entity. In this context, past and present reality was converted into myth.

Confronting Fascist Myths

Rationally conscious processes, normative references, and, more simply, reality checks were a problem for fascists insofar as they established mediations between the inner self and the ultraviolent political conceptions that fascism engendered. In psychoanalytic terms, this fascist process of ideological radicalization of the self could be described as the blurring of distinctions between conscious and unconscious forms of political desire. Whereas Freud saw fascism as an expression of an "atavistic" mentality, fascist theorists seemed to dismiss the subjective possibility, the pluralistic heterogeneity, that psychoanalysis put forward.

Fascism created its own myth of the unconscious. This process of fabrication of the mythical involved specific fascist ideas about the leader, the fascist self, and the state. Moreover, appropriations of history and more classical mythical formations were also primordial to the fascist sense of inner power.

For Freud, a transnational ideology like fascism could be counteracted with an interpretative engagement with the self. In one of his last writings, Freud presented "some elementary lessons in psychoanalysis," concluding that the recognition of the forces of the unconscious did not imply a rejection of being "conscious." As we will see in the next chapter, Freud believed that the psychoanalytic stress on the conscious "remains the one light which illuminates our path and leads us through the darkness of mental life."[21] Unlike the fascists with their mythical idols, Freud believed that reasoned light could, but should not, be instrumentalized by heroes because there was the possibility of creating the conditions for the return of the repressed.[22] Light as carried by the hero creates the conditions for the emergence of its dialectical opposite: darkness.

As in dreams, the fascist and inevitably conscious search for the sources of the unconscious allows a process of reversal, what Freud called the transformation of an element into its opposite. This was, of course, the Freudian lesson for Theodor Adorno and Max Horkheimer's *Dialectic of the Enlightenment*, a process that they described as a regression to barbarism, namely, "the enlightenment's relapse into mythology."[23]

It may be argued that this all-encompassing dialectic was triggered by the effects that fascism was at the time imposing upon modernity. Horkheimer and Adorno even argued that fascism seemed to be a phenomenon that would not vanish with the destruction of the Hitler or Mussolini regimes. Fascism represented an attack against consciousness. In 1944, they contrasted what they hoped would be the brief life of Hitlerism to the *longue durée* of fascist mythmaking. For Adorno and Horkheimer, myths were obscure and luminous at the same time, but they argued that "in fascism . . . conscience is being liquidated."[24]

Freud took the first step in understanding the fascist conflation of history, politics, and mythology, and to some extent his own resistance to fascism became a symptom of this process. He too seemed to believe in the explanatory power of myths. In a book he gave as a present to Mussolini—a "gift" full of analytical implications that I closely analyze in the next chapter—Freud described his approach as "our mythological theory of instincts."[25] Instincts and mythos were also a central aspect of fascist ideology and practice.

In Borges and Freud, as well as in other antifascists theorists like Cassirer, Adorno, Horkheimer, and Gramsci, there is a stark distinction between classical and modern myths. Classical myths appear to be endowed with an authenticity, or even a legitimacy, that antifascist thinkers denied to modern political myths. These political myths became their focus. They presented fascist myths as symptoms of a sort of primordial violence that logos, culture, and reason were previously assumed to have left behind. For Borges and Freud, fascist myths have structural affinities with the ancient mythical world as well as important differences. Classical myths substantially differ from the myth of fascism. The reasons behind these distinctions between old and new myths are many and are interrelated.

The first reason is that classical myths are endowed with a symbolic context that attempts to answer the mystery of being in the world. They provide an explanation of the ultimate reasons of humanity's presence on Earth. The mythology of fascism is equally embedded in the world of eternal fantasy but it also aspires to answer more immediate questions for the present. It does so by attempting the transformation of the mundane politics of the present into a sacred mission. Thus, fascist myths represent a political attempt to conceive politics as faith and the leader as heroic living myth. In this context, for Borges and Freud fascism appears as a religion without legitimacy. In other words, it is a religion that does not seek to contain or restrict itself to calm long-standing existential anxieties; it also wants absolute domination.

The second reason is the difference between the fictitious and the historical nature of its respective leading figures (i.e., Prometheus is not a real person like Hitler). The third reason is that, unlike classical myths, the myths of fascism are not only a product of collective oralities and memories. The process of mythical construction is the result of the conscious will of the leaders. In other words, it is an explicit act of propaganda. This latter aspect, which both Borges and Freud stress, of course contrasts with the fascist arguments highlighting the inner nature of their myths: that is to say, fascists insisted on the unconscious dimension of their movements. The fourth reason, which may seem to contradict the previous ones, is that the myths of fascism generated consensus in the present because they successfully connected with oral memories and myths from the past. They resurfaced mythical undercurrents that were still present in the modern secular world. Fascist myths were standard bearers, by way of reformulation, of a form of primordial mythical thinking that is transhistorical and that a modernity supported by Borges and Freud had delegitimized. Thus, even when it is fabrication the myth of fascism appeals to existing authoritarian longings in society that were not often acknowledged or recognized, and in this way, they can be seen as a new form of politics that implies the return of mythological forces.

In this context, for Borges and Freud classical myths belonged to their past while modern political myths fused artifice with a mythical world of fantasy inspired in the past. This fantasy world appears out of context in the modern and secular present that Borges and Freud defend. The fifth reason is that myth can only be understood from within. If this was possible in the classical world when myths ruled the world through images and emotions, this exercise becomes dangerous or even stupid in the modern world when reason prevails over prejudice. Finally, a sixth difference is of a clear normative nature. While it was legitimized in the imagination and practice of myths in the classical word, violence is ultimately unacceptable in a world ruled by reason. This mythical violence represents a return to barbarism. In Borges and Freud, one can see an agreement on the contextual and intrinsic relation between the displacement from the classical form of myth to the modern political myths and fascism, absolute violence, and racism.

Myth and Irony

The daring ironic, political, and conceptual stance that Freud had with Mussolini in 1933 should not be surprising, coming, as it did, from a master of reading the implicit. In 1937, for example, condensed, conceptually encrypted irony seemed to be the only response to the fascist stress on the death drive. Freud had written to Ernest Jones: "Our political situation seems to become more and more gloomy. The invasion of the Nazis cannot be checked; the consequences are disastrous for analysis as well. The only hope remaining is that one will not live to see it oneself."[26] The carnivalization of hope works here as a symptom of Freud's often melancholic reading of politics. For Freud, fascism represented a turning point in history and a significant challenge to the critical and self-reflective reading of the unconscious that psychoanalysis engendered. As Axel Honneth argues, psychoanalysis represented a self-reflective critical appropriation of the historical. It put forward a critical reading of the past that implied a search for freedom.[27] In this particular sense, one might add that fascism represented an archetypical opposite to freedom. It dissolved the links between past and present and displaced the critical need of working through the past. Fascism abhorred this coming to terms with the past through self-reflection and historical elaboration and it reclaimed the need for a return to myth. According to the fascist view, only myth allowed a more direct, more "authentic" link with the forces of desire in the past and in the present.

Freud saw fascism as replacing the past with its own mythical version of it. The result of this attempt was the projection and actualization of the mythical in the politics of the present. In instrumental terms, this meant, for them, the return of a form of violence rooted in instinctive forces. Fascism conceived this violence as the total essence of being, an unmediated and innate bare violence. In this context, Freud saw this fusion of the mythical with the present as allowing fascism to represent the return of the repressed in politics. He illustrated this situation of the fascist reclamation of the role of the heroic myth of the leader as the mythical return of Prometheus, as I will analyze in the second chapter of the book. With the rise of fascism Prometheus has returned permanently unbound. The past becomes the present, mythical and unmythical. Fascism collapses distinctions. The return of the repressed brings violence, killing, and the unchecked control of the forces of nature (the fire the hero stole from the Gods). The future is opaque. Freud understands the absence of hope in the present as a promise of destruction for the future. As he wrote in 1923: "A great part of my life's work . . . has been spent (trying to) destroy illusions of my own and those of mankind. But if this one hope cannot be at least partly realized, if in the course of evolution we don't learn to divert our instincts from destroying our own kind, If we continue to hate one another for minor differences and kill each other for petty gain, if we go on exploiting the great progress made in the control of natural resources for our mutual destruction, what kind of future lies in store for us?"[28]

Diving into the darkness of the past seemed to be the critical answer for understanding and surviving the collective illusion of fascism. As Eli Zaretsky has suggested, survival and not praise was the overriding motive underling the psychoanalytic reaction vis-à-vis fascism. In this attempt at surviving fascism, psychoanalysis did not refrain from critically analyzing the latter. Psychoanalytic critical thinking "was integral to the great coalition that defeated fascism."[29]

Psychoanalysis is, and certainly was in its prime time, a form of politico-conceptual critique of fascism. Indeed, it was seen as such by fascists. This book reads the perspectives opened by this critical understanding of fascist ideology but also studies fascist understandings of the self and the meaning of myth in politics. Fascism and the Holocaust, and by implication modern forms of genocide and political violence, are rarely studied as the outcome of a transnational ideological current with a strong emphasis on primordial myths, death, sacrifice, and "purification" through violence.

The attempt here is to analyze and contextualize Borges and Freud's shared insistence on the role played by these notions of the mythical self, violence, and the sacred in defining central dimensions of fascism. This is a phenomenon that is not always stressed by historians and critical theorists. The same oversight applies to the analysis of the intellectual reception of the antifascist theory of political myth on both sides of the Atlantic as well as its central role in understanding fascist ideology. In contrast, this book participates in a new trend in studies of Critical Theory, psychoanalysis, fascism, violence, and politics. It complements and expands upon the work of historians and critical theorists that has stressed these relations in order to write new histories and theories of violence.[30]

This book presents different layers of a history of meaning in fascism from the perspectives of Borges and Freud as well as that of the German fascist thinker Carl Schmitt. It is also a contextual critical analysis of, precisely, this fascist sense of meaning, especially according to these distinctive authors. Its chapters stress the centrality that Borges and Freud (and in a very different way Schmitt) ascribed to the role played by the equation of the self, myth, and bare violence in their critical interpretation of fascism.

In its particular analysis, this investigation adopts a transnational perspective that integrates the fields of Critical Theory, European and Latin American history, ideology and politics, the history of racism and anti-Semitism, and Jewish studies. The myth of fascism, or, to put it differently, the essential mythical dimension of fascism, presents a particularly strong case for this kind of transnational analysis. The critical contextualization of Freud, Borges, and Schmitt on the myth of fascism can mutually contribute to the conceptual history of political myth and also to a critical exchange between historiography and theory.

Chapter 2 deals with a key but overlooked moment in the intellectual history of the psychoanalytic reception of fascism and Jewish victimization. By stressing the central, but also opposed, role of myths and heroes for both fascism and psychoanalysis, it presents a contextual and critical reading of Sigmund Freud's interpretations of fascism, Nazism, and anti-Semitism during the 1920s and 1930s.

Chapters 3 and 4 deal with Borges's elaborations on the mythical and "heroic" dimensions of fascism. Conceptual irony was the defining feature of the analytic pessimism that Borges and Freud adopted to read fascist mythology. But in Borges, irony did not only become the object of political and analytical critique; it was also an endless source for his literary genius. For Borges "myth is at the origins of literature but also at its end."[31] It is precisely for this literary reason that for Borges myths do not properly belong to the political field. Myths function in the classical world as collective inventions. They are distorted repositories of memory. With Freud, one could argue that they are imaginary sublimations of primordial violence and that this wording of the myth jumpstarted the processes of pacification of social space. Like Borges, Freud identified these processes with the Enlightenment. Borges agreed with Freud that in the contemporary world of mass politics, the function of the mythical conversely led to the reversal of social pacification: that is to say, it opened the gates to barbarism. Modern political myths promoted war, opprobrium, and a future where life would lose any meaning. Chapter 5 addresses why the opposite was true for Schmitt. For him myth would provide a transcendental meaning where violence, history, and power fully blended. Myth then became a fascist utopia that linked the imaginary past with the future. This idea of a fascism as a mythical utopia was, of course, unpacked by critical antifascists across the Atlantic. Rejecting the empirical past, fascism could only involve the dehumanization (or as Horkheimer and Adorno put it) the loss of the subject via a process of objectification that encapsulated both foundational myth and the myth of reason.

Borges would later return to this topic in his story "Utopia of a Tired Man." For Borges, utopia is a context without a past.

Framed in a future where life ceases to have meaning, the story purposely confuses history with myth. In this dystopian future where history and chronology have been forgotten, only images and glimpses of the past remain. The person inhabiting this future is soon to commit suicide in a gas chamber. We are told that this instrument of death was the gift and legacy of fascism.

—This is the crematorium—Somebody said—The lethal chamber is inside. It is said that it was invented by a philanthropist whose name, I believe, was Adolf Hitler.[32]

In myth, the past is vague and malleable but not the politics of naming that, as Cassirer and, after him, Hans Blumenberg have shown, are central to mythical thinking.[33] Hitler remains a presence in the future where the fragmented memories of the past exist without its history. With subtle irony, Borges equates mythical leadership with nothingness, with a word devoid of historical content where the possibilities of knowledge are minimal. Here myth is identified with the incapacity to think the past in its complex chronological order. In Borges, myth is opposed to history and becomes the object and function of irrational and violent political designs.

Neither Freud nor Borges thinks that reason is fully opposed to myth. Both signal the possibility of thinking the mythical through the real and imagined characters of fascism.

Like their contemporaries Ernst Cassirer, Hannah Arendt, and Adorno and Horkheimer, Borges and Freud agreed on the impossibility of thinking freedom along with overdetermination of the mythical in politics. But in Borges, much more than in Freud, a myth can become the vehicle of conceptual creation, and the heroic myth is especially a motif not only of critique but also of fascination. For Borges, in the realm of literature, the will is full of unconscious mythical dimensions, and can overcome reason. It is only in this realm that the unconscious can achieve a legitimacy that is fully absent for Freud. For Freud, myths and

pathology go hand in hand. In contrast, starting with his reading of Schopenhauer, Borges plays with the idea of an overpowering unconscious individual will as presiding over legitimate
actions. But these actions, as Borges understands them, are non-
political in nature. As we will see in chapter 4, this situation will
become evident in his story "Guayaquil." In that post-1945 story,
Borges returned to the context of fascism and clearly emphasized
the overpowering will of an exiled Jewish historian, Eduardo
Zimmermann. Zimmermann was a fictional character but during the interwar period, Borges had anticipated this approach in
his notable valuation of the Argentine Jewish poet Carlos Grünberg. In 1940, Borges wrote a prologue to Grünberg's book *Mes-
ter de Judería*. For Borges this real Argentine Jewish author
seemed to present a legitimate role for myths that exist at the
antipodes of the political. In other words, he sharply contrasted
Jewish mystical traditions with the political myths of racism. In
both, the real Grünberg and the imaginary Zimmermann, Borges
rescued individual mythical Jewish possibilities for escaping the
furies of fascist politics. This flight from the political was achieved
through poetry (Grünberg) and antiquarian history (Zimmermann). As Borges represented them, neither the real poet nor the
fictional historian was engaged in a form of antifascist thinking
about the effects of the myths of fascism. Unlike Borges himself,
they did not fight back. Their position represents a flight from the
world of fascist fantasy and the reality of the violence it unleashes.
They are stranded in the storm and mystical literature or academic climbing is part of their escapist response. Zimmerman
represents a strong will against the storm, and Grünberg a retreat
into Jewish mysticism. Theirs are individual responses of a non-
political nature. They represent a self that believes in itself but
outside of the antifascist political project. And yet, Borges, like
Freud, does not propose an individualist mystical approach to
question fascist mythology. Myth, and personal intuitive belief
in the self, cannot be the cause and the subjects of resistance to

fascism. In conceptual and also political terms, Borges and Freud question the traditional dichotomy between myth and reason. However, they never abandon the major distinction that opposes one to the other. In fact, they provide a genealogical framework that explains their differences in terms of the potential for immorality in myth and the ethical dimension of reason.

To be sure, class and epochal elitism influenced Borges and Freud, but they were also imbued with a strong emphasis on the plurality of the written word and their own transcendental trust in Enlightenment. Borges and Freud could not bring themselves to think the legitimacy of the mythical in the context of mass politics. They identified their external critique of fascist mythology with a defense of reason. As we will see, Borges would denounce what he saw as a "liberal Jihad" that used and created its own myths to fight fascism. For Borges it was not possible to denounce myth from an equally mythical perspective. Freud thought along the same lines. For both, the myth of fascism is above all a source of trauma and violence. At the center of their arguments lie key questions for us: How is possible to understand the logic of the mythical without assenting to it? Can the written word and rational analysis accurately represent the trauma generated by the myth? If the myth of fascism sublimates violence and transforms mythical ideology into trauma, racism, persecution, torture, and assassination, how reason can understand these processes? Borges and Freud present us with different conceptual paths to think these questions.

Borges, in fact, stresses the ultimate impossibility of representation, and this paradoxically allows his analysis of mythical ideology to reach its most primordial and feral dimensions. Freud, in turn, denies the possibility of an absolute outing of the unconscious as the result of an act of affirming consciousness through interpretation. In the case of the mythical foundations of fascism, the limits of representation are symptoms of the ideological motivation behind them. It is precisely by approaching the limits of the representation of the trauma provoked by the ideology of modern political myth that Borges was able to arrive at a critical interpretation of the mythologies of fascism. "Nazism suffers from irreality," Borges emphasized, pointing to the fascist incapacity to distinguish imaginary from lived experience. The domain of the imaginary gets confused with reality, and what is subjective is objectified through Nazi ideology. According to Hannah Arendt, fascist ideology offers a circular vision of the world. It rejects perception and empirical evidence. By uncritically reiterating its own assumptions, fascism transforms its myths into reality.

For Arendt, fascist ideology is a radical example of the ideological event. Fascism presents its ideology as truth, as an accurate reflection of reality.[34] Reality, in turn, is changed to resemble ideological mandates. Like Arendt during World War II, Borges viewed the absolutist ideology of Nazism as a form of pure violence. In a political "annotation" of 1944, Borges argued that, since Nazism was tantamount to hell, it could not offer a place to live: "it is uninhabitable, men can only die for Nazism, they can lie, kill, and be covered in blood for it."[35] For him, Nazism represents what psychoanalysis calls the death drive. It promises redemption through destruction.

This study of Freud and Borges shows how two very different authors sought to grapple with the problems of representing this primordial mythological horror as it was converted into reality by global fascism. Unlike Freud, Borges, by then an antifascist Argentine writer, did not observe the events leading to the unfolding of the Holocaust firsthand, but he bore witness to it from distant Buenos Aires, where a local fascist movement was ascendant. Significantly, his peripheral position prompted Borges to consider the global dimensions of the fascist politics of the mythical self and its deadly effects. As a writer, he often developed these two different subject positions of victims and perpetrators as a way to make sense of their distinctive experiences.

As we will see in this book, Borges's portrayals are uncannily effective in terms of what the philosopher María Pía Lara has called the disclosive potential of certain narratives. Such texts generate reflective judgments. Furthermore, through their capacity to thematize the myth of fascism, and, more specifically, to imaginatively convey through language the extreme nature of genocidal atrocities, they enhance our comprehension of history.[36] Although he never saw a Nazi extermination camp, at the time of the Shoah Borges displayed a firm grasp of the ideological and mythical ramifications of the annihilation of European Jewry.

This is the first book in any language to examine the converging critical perspectives of Freud and Borges on genocidal trauma and fascist mythical violence. Placing their writings in their national and international contexts offers a historical understanding of the global ramifications of the myth of fascism.

Scholars of history and theory, fascism, and the Holocaust and anti-Semitism might well be surprised by this relational focus on Freud and Borges, just as scholars of Borges and Freud might be surprised when I analyze their works through the analytical frames of Critical Theory, Holocaust historiography, and studies of transnational fascism. But, in fact, Freud and Borges were analytical pioneers in the understanding of fascism as the problematic culmination of the history of myth in its political displacement from the classic world to modernity. In Freud's case, persecution and exile allowed him to have a marginal view of the early stages of a genocidal process in which Freud, like most of the victims, were powerless. In the case of Borges, the peripheral view of an Argentina that was at the same time provincial and cosmopolitan opened wide interpretative possibilities. These openings were much more uncommon among his European and American peers.

In making this claim, I do not mean that Europe, Critical Theory, fascism, or the Holocaust need to be "provincialized" in

terms of the views of these two antifascist intellectuals or that
European events can only be explained in terms of postcolonial
realities or vice versa. But I do maintain that certain postcolonial studies have shown that the local and the global are mutually inclusive. In the case of modern genocide, for example, Nazi
concentration and extermination camps are part of the genealogy of the modern age's "carceral archipelagos" of victimization.[37]
Moreover, witnessing and interpreting the connections between
ideology, myth, and trauma blur conventional geopolitical distinctions between European and Latin American history, modern Jewish history, as well as other histories. To put it another
way, we may well see the center more clearly from the margins.[38]

Unlike Borges, who imagined exile through a character, the
Jewish historian Zimmermann in his story "Guayaquil," Freud
was actually affected by political exile. However, the connection
between exile and thinking politics from the antifascist margins
was a fate that Borges shared with Freud and it became indeed a
central dimension of their conceptual experience of thinking fascism from political peripheries. As Michael Steinberg suggests
with respect to Freud's last years as experienced in *Moses and
Monotheism*, "The survival of subjectivity in exile is enabled by
the definition of subjectivity as exile. The reader must then decide
whether this position is to be understood as a function of personal
exile and old age, in other words as a contingency and a symptom, or whether the position, in its very embrace of its own contingency and symptomaticity, catches a basic reality of modern
subjectivity enabled by the clairvoyance of Sigmund Freud in
contemplation of fascism and its threat to human dignity."[39]
Symptoms and insights are interwoven in the web of interpretation that this book studies. In this context Borges's case is analyzed in chapters 3 and 4. The chapters deal with the Argentine
writer's critical insights on the mythical and unconscious dimensions of fascist politics for they provide a unique synthesis of the
fascist politics of desire. There is a sense in which Borges became

himself a symptom of the resistance to fascism, but he also transcended this resistance with his unique stress on the self-reflective dimensions of the democratic culture that fascism attempted to destroy. For Borges in 1944, the explanation of fascism was rooted, in part, in mythical notions of a heroic self. Borges was not an exception among critical antifascist thinkers at the time but he was able to recognize key dimensions of fascism that were apparently voided to many others.

Borges converged with Freud in a critical theorization of fascist myths but he was not broadly influence by his thinking. In this sense, Borges differed from significant theorists of modern political myth such as the antifascists Mariátegui, Adorno and Horkheimer, and Ernst Cassirer.

Psychoanalysis, like fascism, crossed the Atlantic and traveled the world. Jürgen Habermas has noted that in the 1920s and 1930s "there was no theory of contemporaneity not affected to its core by the *penetrating force of fascism*."[40] In particular, Habermas has in mind those theorists that shared a "fascinated excitement" with the fascist matter. But as he also suggests, Critical Theory was also affected by it. It was precisely this confrontation of Critical Theory with fascism that shaped a broad spectrum of critical thinkers of fascist mythology in Europe, Latin America, the United States, and beyond.

This book represents an attempt to rethink fascist and totalitarian theories of political myth in terms of the perspectives opened by Freud's and Borges's own understanding of death, desire, and fascist processes of victimization.

From the perspective of psychoanalysis, fascism presented a transnational alternative to Freudian psychology.[41] Fascism had an entirely different conception of the unconscious both as a source political knowledge and as the ultimate reflection of fascist authenticity. Freud and Borges critically and acutely observed this distinction. With its emphasis on the unconscious, but also on repression and culture, psychoanalysis challenged the fascist transposition of the mythical and the fascist conception of the self. And by resorting to its basic transnational nature, they presented a global conceptual alternative across nations and continents. From Germany and Italy to Brazil, Argentina, and beyond, psychoanalysis engaged fascism and vice versa. This was a conceptual global discussion as well as a political one. To be sure, Freud's at times transhistorical understanding of fascism limited his understanding of the changing historical nature of fascist ideology. But ironically it was perhaps this limited contextual engagement that enabled him to "read" structural elements of fascist ideology and its connections to both barbarism and civilization.

Fascists across the Atlantic clearly saw this situation. This was both a practical threat and a theoretical one. Even before the famous anti-Semitic campaigns in Italy and Germany and elsewhere in Europe after 1939, which unsurprisingly conflated psychoanalysis with Judaism and Marxism, some fascists noticed the critical antifascist dimensions of psychoanalytic thinking.

Benito Mussolini himself wondered about the scientific status of psychoanalysis and posed that it was an "imposture." Nonetheless, the Duce suggested that psychoanalysis could be used to understand the internal logic of communism as a political pathology. Thus, for him an illegitimate and pathological corpus such as Freudian theory could be used to understand the unhealthy nature of communism. For Mussolini, as for many other fascists, psychoanalysis was the product of a rational mentality that fascism regarded as a disease of the mind. For this reason, it could only be used with the enemy but not to understand normal people such as himself and other fascists. Moreover, for many fascists such as the Argentine cleric-fascist Father Virgilio Filippo, Freud was a living example of the disease that he was studying and thus was able to understand so well. In short, he accused Freud of understanding a false myth from within.[42] In turn, Mussolini stated that psychoanalysis could explain the division within the left, and especially the mentality of the Amedeo Bordiga faction that published the magazine *Prometheus* in Italy.

Those antifascists that denied the mythical truth of fascism used a classical myth to present their fight, or, as the Duce suggested (adopting another mythical image), to present a "communist labyrinth," a fact that could not have escaped Mussolini. That Freud was Jewish also did not escape Mussolini. Many fascists writing on psychoanalysis started their consideration of psychoanalysis by noticing Freud's ethnic identity. Like Mussolini, the fascist Alberto Spaini had presented Freud as a false Jewish intellectual that wanted to "pontificate."[43] Mussolini called "the Viennese Jewish Professor Freud" the "Maximus pontifice" of Psychoanalysis.[44] Incapable of establishing any dialogue with psychoanalytic critique, the Duce presented Freud as the leader of false myth or even a fake religion. In this sense, one may argue that for Mussolini, Freud epitomized the antithesis of his sacralizing mythical leadership. For fascism, its own myth represented the truth. It was not a metaphor or the naturalized expression of political fights that occurred throughout history but the natural outcome of the collective will.

In Argentina, the fascist poet Leopoldo Lugones presented psychoanalysis as the fundamental element of a modern philosophy that questioned the legitimacy of myth and the principles of order and authority that emanated from it.

Borges would later observe this centrality of political myth, in his own book titled *Leopoldo Lugones* (1960), where Borges dealt with an author that had been so influential for him but that he also rejected politically. For Borges, Lugones was "the apostle of the hour of the sword," the prophet of violence. Borges observed that Lugones's genuine interest in classical mythology led him to rethink its political potential for the modern period. He wanted to establish a modern mythology for the Argentine nation. Borges read him correctly. In his book *Prometeo* (1910),

Lugones had already blurred the distinction between logos and mythos by clearly stating that classical myths constituted the foundation of Argentina and Latin American nations. For Lugones, ancient myths not only shaped the origins of the present but also established connections between the historical facts and transhistorical truths. This belief in the historical truth of myth rendered history into a realm of fantasy and, later in his life, would lead Lugones to develop fascism the Argentine way, namely, clerico-fascism. Borges presented this form of fascism as "the totalitarian creed of Lugones [el credo totalitario de Lugones]."[45] In this theoretical context, for Lugones Freud had perpetrated an unacceptable artificial critique of myth. He had questioned the sacred dimension of the political theology that the poet defined as the true form of fascism: Argentine *nacionalismo*.

By denying the sacred dimension of fascism and by presenting it as the return of a Western form of barbarism, Freud was essentially opposed to fascism. If for Lugones myths defined the best of the West, Freud put into question the very notion of the divine and even framed these fantasies historically as being rooted in the mythical words of instincts. Lugones stated " 'God is [for *Freud*] no more than the idealization, in itself bipolarized, of the *Totem* or beast-pet that some savage tribes possess."[46]

Whereas Lugones desired the political reactualization of the classic, and for him authoritarian, legacy of Greek myths, Freud highlighted how these desires were pathologically located in a world of pain. For Lugones, Freud represented an "antireligion." While Lugones regarded psychoanalysis as above all "anti-Christian," he advocated for a fascist and Christian Argentina.

From the perspective of fascism, psychoanalytic theory represented a politico-conceptual critique of fascism. If fascism ultimately relied on an uncomplicated notion of the self as a source of inner authenticity, psychoanalysis put into question the most basic assumptions of fascist theory.

The work of Freud was not central to Italian fascist ideology, but Mussolini and other fascists read Freudian texts in ways that provide a unique window onto the understanding of this ideology, specifically with respect to fascist theories of myth. Within a contextual analysis of fascist theory and its related modes of interpretation, the book analyzes two different antifascist perceptions of political myth. To be sure, fascists discussed different modes of interpreting their counterrevolution but they all emphasized the role of what, following Freud's interpretation of fascism, Adorno called "the fascist unconscious."[47]

The fascist unconscious could not be anything but opposed to psychoanalytic theory. In sharp contrast to the Italian case, psychoanalysis was a central element of the fascist conception of the enemy in Borges's Argentina.

As Borges and Freud understood so well, seeing fascism implies looking at the collapse of rational thinking, namely, the negative resolution of the conflict between instinctual drives and the demands of civilization. In this context, political hope seemed evanescent. But its turning upside down, through a dense critical theory full of ironic condensation, led to the reassertion of ethico-political choices and democratic imperatives in the context of political oppression and contemporary political mythologies.[48] In other words, the critical theorists that this book analyzes sought to interpret the unconscious sources of fascist politics as well as how the fascists understood them in mythical terms. The result of this theoretical confrontation with fascist theories led to a more critical awareness of the contextual implications of mythic politics. These were the sources of the dialectic disruption facing the Kantian cosmopolitan project.[49]

Freud saw this critique as the affirmation of life, even in death. In a critically dangerous situation, and after the Nazis had annexed Austria, Freud had equally addressed the German fascists as symptoms of the reversal of the civilizing process. Before letting the Freuds leave the country, the Gestapo insisted that he sign a statement that they had not ill-treated them. He signed, adding the comment: "I can most highly recommend the Gestapo to everyone."[50] Freud had a few minutes to think and yet he delivered. Indeed, he told the Nazis, as he had told Mussolini, that they meant destruction.

All in all, it is with critical irony and analytical condensation that Freud, and also Borges, thought fascism as the overpowering rule of mythology in politics. Irony, and with it the Freudian and Borgean drives to think beyond the explicit, escapes many historians in the present as it escaped fascism in the past. But fascism did not escape their critical gaze. The Argentine fascists frequently questioned Borges. Freud was persecuted by German fascism. It remains the task of interpreters to recognize the critical potential of the Freudian and Borgean prisms that so many fascists perceived at the time, when, in the case of Freud, they were burning his books. The horizon of possibilities opened by this recognition was, and perhaps should still be, a source for a self-reflective historical critique of fascism.

{ 2 }

Freud, Fascism, and the Return of the Myth

The Id and the super-ego have one thing in common: they both represent the influences of the past.

—SIGMUND FREUD, 1938-1939

IN EARLY 1933 SIGMUND FREUD received an inconvenient visitor. The visitor was Giovachino Forzano, a renowned fascist opera composer and a personal friend of Benito Mussolini. Forzano's daughter was a patient of Edoardo Weiss, the noted Italian psychoanalyst. A Freudian loyalist, Weiss wanted Freud's personal supervision of the case and he went to the Austrian capital, taking with him his patient and her fascist father. The three distinctive individuals showed up at Freud's home on Berggasse 19 on April 26, 1933, and the fascist Forzano asked Freud to dedicate one of his books to Mussolini.[1]

Freud found himself in a difficult position, a double bind of sorts. If he dedicated a book to the Duce, he would be defined as a fascist fellow traveler or worse. But if he decided not to do so, he would probably endanger the already difficult standing of Italian psychoanalysts vis-à-vis the fascist regime.[2] Moreover, Freud was quite aware of the fact that, at this time, Mussolini stood as a "protector" against the Nazis at home (in Austria) and abroad.[3]

Almost three months before Forzano's visit, Hitler had become the chancellor of Germany. Hitler had full-fledged anti-Semitic goals, or, as Freud put it, Nazism meant violence with a program "whose only political theme is pogroms."[4]

Freud wrote in his dedication to Mussolini: "To Benito Mussolini, with regards from an old man that recognizes in the ruler the Hero of Culture."[5]

Did really Freud consider Mussolini his hero? Some years before, in 1928, he had expressed in a private letter his extreme dislike for Mussolini.[6] Many historians have famously presented Freud as being inward-looking vis-à-vis Austrian and European polities, holding an escapist attitude toward politics. As Carl Schorske argues in his classic study, psychoanalysis was born as a result of a Freudian displacement, from the reality of politics to the workings of the mind.[7] To be sure, Freud thought that his "science" of psychoanalysis was a life-fulfilling creation that transcended nations, political cultures, and identity formations. Thus, he often relegated politics to the contingency of (historical) external life, whereas, for him, the study of the workings of the mind linked these historical elements with transhistorical ones. This argument is important and deserves consideration. But there is a political dimension of psychoanalysis that many authors focusing on the "liberal" German elements of Freud's personality tend to downplay.[8]

Freud may have escaped from actual politics but politics did not escape him. There is an emancipatory, almost utopian, dimension in Freud's thinking that includes but also goes beyond his own Austrian national context.[9] Like many of his contemporaries, Freud had a transnational antifascist understanding of global political processes that went beyond restrictive notions of his many identities.[10] It is actually the productive combination of all these subject positions (being Austrian and living in a baroque Catholic environment, being European, being Jewish, being antifascist, being a scientist) that disabled Freud's encounter with identity politics (and the mythical foundations underlying them) and displaced him to the significations of actual politics. Freud enacted, practically and theoretically, the position of the outsider. He dedicated the last years of his life to tracing the political dimensions of desire. For him, these dimensions were in turn engendered by heroic and primordial myths. His last book, *Moses and Monotheism* (1939), epitomizes this Freudian search for meaningful answers in the history of individual and collective leadership, that is to say, the history of politics. Behind the founding traumas of Judaism (that is, behind the symptom), Freud was able to read the political. In this sense, the political dimension was not an absence, an abstract source of metahistorical considerations, but a palpable historical loss.[11] It was not an excuse for political retreat but a pathway of antifascist engagement.

The political dimension, the Freudian recognition of personal and collective powerlessness in front of fascism, was a central, if not the central, frame of reference for Freud's last years. To be sure, he actually described in 1933 to Ernest Jones a personal feeling of numbness that was provoked by "the bleak misery of these times which at present stifles all more meaningful activity for me."[12] But, as I will demonstrate, Freud was not exclusively engaged in melancholic detachment. Throughout the context of the ideological civil war of the interwar years, Freudian psychoanalysis represented an effort in political understanding.[13] Like antifascism at large, psychoanalysis defined its political place as the result of an act of disempowerment, namely, a subject position affected by the losses provoked by persecution and victimization. Psychoanalysis's early status as a "pariah," its almost constitutive condition of internal exile and academic displacement, provided a precedent as well as a conceptual framework to the antifascist perspective of exile.[14] Moreover, it was theoretically suited to analyzing fascist aggression as constitutive of the fascist notion of politics as mythology. Freud was quite aware, as we will see, of fascist processes of demonization and he saw them as radical outcomes of modernity's propensity to open up to the historical, as well as mythical, forces of destruction that had preceded it. Being an expert in the analysis of myths, Freud confronted the founding political myths of fascism throughout the interwar years and especially in his work *Moses and Monotheism*.[15]

Freud's own encounter with Mussolini, Hitler, and, more generally, fascism was informed by this active political dimension that Freud could not escape. Psychoanalysis, in its encounter with fascism, became a form of antifascism. It was not the antifascism of the "established" intellectuals but the antifascism of the outsiders with no place in society or culture or politics.[16]

Early on, Freud saw the uttermost consequences of destructive drives in politics. The fascist leader is a radical narcissist that wishes to be loved outside the limits of the law. Fascism provides its own self-centered definition of transcendence as the politicization of the heroic classical myth and its transposition into a novel form of the totalitarian politics of violent and primordial drives. In this framework, the will of the leader appears as the embodiment of the paternal metaphor. This idea of the will represents what Freud described as "omnipotence of thoughts," based on an overestimation of the influence the self "can exert on the outer world by changing it." Freud argued that this mindset was typical "in our children, adult neurotics, as well as in primitive people."[17] As is the case with them, fascism, unaffected by the reality principle, refuses the power of discourse, of dialogue and language, and proposes sacrifice and violence as the means and ends for achieving its political cult.[18]

There is much truth to the notion that the fascist leader thinks in terms of circular images, reifies ritual, and radicalizes the political value of performance.[19] But the fascist persuasion was for Freud more importantly embedded in history than in aesthetics or performance. Freud confronted fascism with contextualization. Like Hannah Arendt, another great interpreter of fascism, Freud opposed mythical thinking in politics with the capacity to think.[20] But Freud was very different from Arendt. To be sure, she identified the myth as a lie and also considered lies to be the constitutive sources of fascism. However, she never developed a critique of the mythical dimensions of fascism.[21] In contrast, Freud adopted a combination of critical irony and an analytical form of condensation in historically analyzing myths of origins. His view was full of transhistorical elements that Freud used from the vantage point of their metaphorical value. Critical irony could be defined as a reassertion of the capacity to think when confronted with a circular vision of the world, a full-fledged totalitarian ideology. Condensation provides the possibility of using analogy by focusing on an object of symbolic analogical power. But what are the limits of a criticism when the subject of the critique, the one who is being criticized, cannot understand or even be recognized as such? Do implicit, or even cryptic, political statements such as we saw in the case of Freud's "dedication" to Mussolini represent a form of resistance? Freud provided a conceptual metaphorics of fascism through critical irony and analytical condensation rather than through systematic argumentation. In other words, he presented a language for understanding and surviving fascism, a language full of emancipatory potential.[22]

If fascism put forward a notion of politics as the realm of collective psychology and as an attempt to master individual wills, Freud thought that the fascist attempt to provide closure to political utopias could be only understood in terms of a transhistorical longing to return to a primeval state. Both fascism and psychoanalysis put forward transhistorical and transnational notions of political desire. But whereas Mussolini conceived desire, particularly his own, to be a political imperative that transcended history and national territories, Freud conceived fascism as the return of a mythical past, particularly that represented by heroic myths such as the one of Prometheus. He actually put forward this interpretation in his dedication to Mussolini but this was not apparent. I will return to Prometheus in the next section of this chapter, but first we will deal with the different intellectual paths traversed by Freud's conception of fascism. Literally, these were the Freudian inroads into the understanding of transnational fascism.

When confronted with Forzano's impending fascist request to address the Duce, Freud, a master of reading the implicit, preferred to face off with the Duce with apparent praise and encrypted radical critique. Connecting Mussolini with historical examples, or even with explicit Greek myths, was out of the question. It would have been too obvious.

Freud gave to Forzano, and Mussolini, a book that was full of intertextual implications. It was a copy of a pacifist book published that year—coauthored with Albert Einstein, the book was titled *Why War?* Freud gave to Mussolini a book that, as he once noted, was forbidden in Nazi Germany![23] To Mussolini, the man who famously claimed that war, in its ultimate accomplishment of radical violence, was the essence of fascism, he gave a book that presented war as the reification of death, an example of the "blindness to logic."[24]

Freud suggested that Mussolini was a hero of civilization or, as he put it, a "cultural hero." In this chapter, I provide a close reading of this dedication in terms of its encrypted, and often cryptic, connections to broader dimensions of the Freudian corpus. Equally important, I will put this dedication in context.

As Mussolini and Forzano did, many historians of fascism have misread Freud's "dedication" to the Duce. They failed, so to speak, to see behind the deliberate or the symptom. By reading Freud's dealing with Mussolini in literal terms, they have overlooked the essential contribution of psychoanalytic thinking to the understanding of fascism and, last but not least, they have missed Freud's own contribution to antifascism as a political ideology.[25] Was psychoanalysis compatible with fascism? Was Freud sympathetic to fascism as other historians would claim? All these questions are related to or even framed by another question that is perhaps more significant: What is the ideological connection between fascism and psychoanalysis? In other words: Where are these two "philosophies," or focal systems of understanding, affected by each other?[26] That psychoanalysis was against fascism the Nazis knew well. One week after Freud had received Forzano, the Nazis were burning Freud's books all over Germany while stating that Nazism was against the "soul-disintegrating exaggeration of the instinctual life" that psychoanalysis represented.[27] Irony once more seemed to be Freud's best answer to universal fascism. When confronted with Nazi book burning, he stated, "What progress we are making. In the Middle Ages they would have burnt me: nowadays they are content with burning my books."[28]

The carnivalization of the outsider transformed his books into real subjects of a textual pogrom. This was a fascist instrumental displacement: Freud, the person, became objectified and his books became sacrificial subjects. But for Freud, fascism was not exclusively, or even principally, medieval. Freud presented the historical condition of fascism as a reformulation of the past in the present. Thus, fascism was not derivative of the past but a radical interpretation of it. Hitler, of course, referred to the medieval and Christian tradition of anti-Semitism as a precursor to his own racism.[29]

Freud put forward the possibility of a reinstantiation of the classic heroic myth in Christianity. Mythology was latent in Christian monotheism. He emphasized the Nazi and fascist links with the metamorphosis of the primordial myth in Christianity, as it had existed in Europe. Europeans had been " 'badly christened'; under the thin veneer of Christianity they have remained what their ancestors were, barbarically polytheistic."[30] This was for Freud one of the reasons for fascist anti-Semitism, and, like fascism at large, it was rooted in the contradiction between monotheism and polytheism.

As Freud ironically wrote to a disciple exiled in Palestine: "Have you read that Jews in Germany are to be forbidden to give their children German names? They can only retaliate by demanding that the Nazis refrain from using the popular names of John, Joseph, and Mary."[31] The idea of ironic retaliation speaks to the profound sense of critical powerlessness. Only rational engagement and ironic condensation provided solace and, more importantly, understanding of the place and power of myth in fascism.

The general antifascist idea that fascism represented the past, namely, that it was rooted in a barbaric past, explicitly contradicted Mussolini's famous dictum that fascism, like history, did not "travel backwards."[32] But for Freud, unlike many other antifascists, the relationship between fascism and the past was not the result of a mimetic identification or mere derivation. To be sure, fascism was "reactionary" and "medieval,"[33] but more importantly it equally presented a novel articulation of the myths of the past. Moreover, Freud saw the fascist connection with the past as a combination of historical experiences and collective mythical frameworks that preceded history. Most significantly, Freud believed that humanity's earlier moments were represented by myths. Myths represented the structural foundations of society. Myths represented history before it became properly historical. The past began as a transhistorical reality. In Freud's view of the past, the relation between close and remote is blurred.[34] There is no single date, or period, for a myth insofar as the myth "happened" at the founding moments of human development, namely, before history. The myth was a response to the founding trauma of human society.[35] But what was the connection between this idea of the past and Freud's understanding of fascism as rooted in the past? Fascism was encompassed not only by its historical past but also by mythical connotations. For Freud, myths are not so much metaphors for explaining fascism but rather constitute its rooted unconscious. Before turning to this key dimension of Freud's interpretation of fascism, I will briefly explore the fascist idea of consciousness.

Fascist "Consciousness"

In fascism, consciousness was not a repression of inwardness (as Freud understood the workings of the Ego toward the Id) but its actual distillation. The idea that superior innate instincts constituted the roots of being conscious was not obviously explained but was presented in fascism as an objective moment of self-recognition. This search for the authenticity of the self was an act of "revelation." The discipline and hierarchies that this recognition supposedly generated constituted fascism and their outcomes were "the primitive and exalted consciousness of fascists."[36] Fascism returned individuals to their primitive genuineness. This authenticity was essentially antidemocratic. In fascism, "the antidemocratic spirit is developed with full consciousness."[37]

Fascist consciousness was above all defined by compulsion and not by reason. Ironically, the act of searching the fascist soul could not be an unconscious mechanical process but a conceptual exercise. In this context and without noting the necessary mediation of language, fascists claimed that Mussolini's words were fused with action insofar as they "precede, announce, register, and determine the facts."[38]

More generally for fascists, words were diametrically opposed to their movement. The doctrine emanated from "facts more than words." The "action and the spirit" defined the fascist revolutionary subject.[39] Words ruled in liberalism.[40] In fascism, concepts, words, and symbols did not truly represent objects or subjects. Their original function in a symbolic order was rather replaced with words that were supposed to be verbal incarnations for fascist actions. "Words first should be flesh, that is life." Only after being embedded in historical processes could their leader's words assume a representational role.[41] By fully knowing the contours of the national soul, the fascist unconscious led to consciousness as the fascists understood it. It was then that fascists talked of achieving political freedom. And it was then that they talked of the creation of a "new fascist consciousness."[42]

This state of consciousness was not contemplative but similar to that of a sublime sensation of ecstasy. This dimension was often noted by both fascists and nonfascists alike. Mussolini argued, "One cannot understand anything that is great without being in a state of lovely passion, in a state of religious mysticism."[43] To be sure, Mussolini also argued that reasoning was equally important. But the idea of reasoning was itself related to the fascist notion of experience in the context of ecstatic understanding. Rooted in subjectivity, the "fascist mystique" linked the individual to the collective. It was a "totalitarian mystique" precisely because, at the same time that it denied "inhuman leveling," it placed individuals vis-à-vis the fascist state and its leader, and it did so through a religious sense of urgency.[44]

Fascism represented the original simplicity of feelings. As Rocco put it, "fascism is merely *unconscious nationalism*."[45] The Others, those who were opposed to fascism, were lacking a true consciousness; they were devoid of potency as it emerged from the souls of fascists.

As the fascist Fernando Mezzasoma put it, as a result of this youthful affirmation of life, potency, and domination, fascist Italy "walks against everything and against everyone."[46]

This truth embodied violent, militaristic, and imperialist feelings. Imperialism especially represented the national projection of collective feelings of potency, what Mussolini often called the will to dominate. As Mussolini put it in 1919, "imperialism represents the foundation of life for every people that tend to expand economically and spiritually."[47] That same year, he added that imperialism was the "eternal and immutable law of life." It represented the "need, the desire, and the will of expansion that every individual, that every vital people (popolo) has in itself."[48]

Fascism represented the "return of full and whole life to politics." Fascism was a "military and warrior Risorgimento." In turn, fascist imperialism would represent the collective "will of potency." As the nationalist and eventually fascist Enrico Corradini presented it, it was "a doctrine of life" against death. The life of instincts acted against decadence, specifically against political formations like liberalism and socialism (which he called "parasites"), and it would return Italians to the cult of heroes. For Corradini, once this "will of potency" prevailed, myths would become "real and true."[49]

The fascist links with this past were organic but also psychological. As Arrigo Solmi put it, fascism represented "an instinctive synthesis of national defense founded in national consciousness." This consciousness had been "revealed" to the people who relied on the organic forces of their race. Here revelation was tantamount to political introspection. The importance of fascism was not related to the creation of a "new economic or social doctrine." Its centrality lay "in the quasi-instinctive synthesis of a complex of doctrines and actions aimed at saving the new civil society" from internal and external dissolving forces. In short, fascism was naturally linked to Italian history insofar as "it had known how to gather and bring to light the essence by unconsciously deriving it from the living sources of tradition."[50]

Fascism returned the repressed mythical past to politics. It represented "the voice and the will of the stirpe," as Augusto Turati (secretary general of the Fascist Party from 1926 to 1930) argued in 1928.[51] Like Turati and many other fascists, the fascist intellectual Camilo Pellizzi opposed life and hierarchy to a democratic order of nations and collectives. Fascist politics were authentic because they were rooted in nature. "We are against liberalism but have an extremely violent and almost physiological sense of freedom."[52] But this freedom was very specific and extremely limited for most fascists. It was not the "abstract" and "negative" freedom of democracy but the freedom of the "will." Against the "subjective" understanding of freedom, fascism proposed the "positive" and "concrete" freedom of life under dictatorship. Life was then repositioned in a natural order of things. Hierarchy and authority belonged to this natural order. In dictatorship, freedom could be "built" objectively. In dictatorship, "consciousness" was no longer "isolated." Freedom was no longer "subjective" but objectified as recognition of a "rational will."[53]

Fascist consciousness represented the outing of the fascist unconscious. For fascists, it was only then, when reason was pushed aside, that the self was truly free. Here rationality did not mean reason but rather its submission to the desires of the soul.

For example, in 1936 when empire as a sentiment was finally incarnated in reality, Luigi Federzoni argued that when the people enthusiastically shouted "Duce! Duce! Duce!," after Mussolini had given Italy an empire, they were expressing deep ideological patterns. In these shouts, he said, "the superb sentiment of a people vibrated. The sentiment of a people finally revealed to itself. They demonstrated the feelings of a people that is conscious of being masters of its future, sure of its force." The fascist empire represented the "obstinate will to live" of the people. They were fused in a "compact . . . victory-block of souls under the guidance of the Duce." All the force of history had sided with Italians against the "antihistory [*antistoria*]."[54] The link between the leader and history was full of mythical elements. Locating its origins in the past was the key to follow the myth of the present. Hitler had maintained that his own personification of racial myths was an epochal change. The Führer stated in *Mein Kampf* that the Arian "is the Prometheus of mankind, from whose bright forehead the divine spark of genius has sprung at all times."[55] This Arian Prometheus was the hero that "forever kindling anew that fire of knowledge . . . illumined the night of silent mysteries and thus caused man to climb the path to mastery over the other beings of this earth." In typical projective mode, Hitler warned against the exclusion of this prototypical man, "exclude him and perhaps after few thousand years darkness will again descend on the earth, human culture will pass, and the world turn to a desert." Hitler divided humanity in three groups, the "founders of culture," the "bearers of culture," and the "destroyers of culture," and stated that only the Aryan could be considered a creator of culture. Hitler conflated the fire bringer with Arian supremacy. The Aryan Prometheus became the mythical foundation for racial domination.

For one of his biographers, in his revolutionary age, Mussolini had been a young "Prometheus." Creation and revelation marked the affinity between the dictator and the titan: "Mussolini had created a new civilization" and had "communicated to humanity extraordinary and profound secrets as Prometheus had communicated fire."[56] This idea of the fascist leader incarnating older classical myths was central to fascism as an ideology, movement, and regime. This is what Freud meant in his encrypted dedication to Mussolini.

Freud, Fascism, and the Dictatorship of the Mind

Fascism presented a tension between its radical nationalism and its transnational dimensions (its imperialist pan-national ideology). Fascist imperialism, for example, is central to any understanding of these transnational features.[57] Although his analysis was essentially transnational, Freud did not consider this dimension. He often presented Nazism as "German fascism" or presented the Austrian fascists as being "cousins" of German fascism.[58] Fascism transcended national borders and even at one point constituted a fascist international, but for Freud fascist transcendence laid elsewhere. Fascism was a global phenomenon, but besides its cross-border affinities and reformulations, Freud saw fascism as the transhistorical substantiation of a mythical past: namely, fascism was a repetition, a novel version of the myth of the primordial father.

Thus, the father figure represents the prerational and precivilizational world of images, that is, the dominion of the visual over the written word. For example, Nazism's declared anti-Jewish nature and, last but not least, its repetitive burning of texts by Jewish authors represented for Freud a confirmation of a long cultural battle between image and language. This was a battle that paganism and Judaism came to epitomize. It is not that Judaism was against any image per se. But the attribution of divine power to a given image runs counter to a longstanding Jewish tradition, namely, the sublimation of desire through language. It is language, the text, that allows us access to the sacred. The Jewish injunction against the visual representation of desire was a central dimension of psychoanalysis. For the historian Michael Steinberg, psychoanalysis is a critical engagement that confronts "the duality of a regime of ideology and a regime of representation, whose power and authority are to be penetrated through the counteroffensive of analysis. Manifest content thus cedes its power to the latent at the same time, at least in dreams, that vision and images cede their authority to text. What is latent, what is unconscious, carries too much meaning to be permitted to cross the barrier into the conscious or the manifest without disguise and distortion. Its content is historical violence."[59]

Historical violence, as well as its visual representation, becomes the object of psychoanalytic critique. Whereas Freud saw Greek myths or historical leaders like Caesar, Napoleon, Hitler, and Mussolini as representing a full aesthetic renunciation of ethics, he considered Moses to represent reason, the triumph of ideas and ethics over performance and images. Moses was, for Freud, a source of intellectual and historical resistance: namely, he represented life against the forces of destruction.[60]

Moses's program was based not on instincts and rituals of violence (such as premodern pogroms) but on scripture. In short, it was based on an idea and a concept rather than on an image or a feeling. The image claims to embody the actual presence of the Freudian primordial father whereas language is represented by the displacement of the father figure onto the normative aspects of civilization. The brief rapture of violence, the return of the repressed presented in the breaking of the tables of the law— Moses's violent (irrational) reaction against the image of the divinity represented in the golden calf—shows for Freud the labile nature of rational engagement. Even Moses was tempted to destroy the books of law, and replace language with violence. Freud, of course, identified Nazi book burning with mythical atavism.

For Freud, the Christian religion and a European historical experience (the armies of Caesar and Napoleon) represented a return of the primordial father. But unlike the question of religion, and as with Caesar and Napoleon, fascism presented the persona of the hero (the leader) as an immediate presence. Freud was interested in historical leaders, what his disciple and biographer Ernst Jones called "leaders of men." Accordingly, Moses, Napoleon, Caesar, Hannibal, and other leaders epitomize the repetitive return of the father.[61]

As is well known, incest lays at the center of the most important mythical engagement of psychoanalysis: the Oedipus complex.[62] Some historians argue that the Oedipus complex works as metaphor for Freud's own personal retreat from the practice of politics. It should be no surprise then that Freud may have also interpreted politics through this lens. The assassination of the primordial father represented a source of emasculation, the "precipitate" reflected in the Greek or Incan myths that allowed normativity and unchecked violence to stop. In short, civilization, or the "cultural process," was based on the renunciation of desire. It rested on the rejection, and displacement, of the desire to kill as well as on the negative drive to follow a primordial father, a totemic figure that had tyrannical dimensions. A symbol of this renunciation is the democratic sublimation of the killing of the father as a rejection of strong political leadership. Civilization rests in part on this "cultural frustration."[63]

In Freudian terms, a dictatorship is directed against this democratic sublimation and its consequential renunciation of destructive forces. The return of the father, the violent leader, encompassed a return to "primitive" unmediated violence and the renunciation of norms, namely, a rejection of civilization. As a leader, Moses may have been a father figure, but Freud presented the existence of many Moseses as proof that mediation and symbolism were not lost but innate to Judaism or, at least, to Freud's own reading of it. Here Judaism, of course, represented a symptom of the possibilities for normative progressive civilization.

Freud saw Christianity as more syncretically related to paganism than to Judaism. The baroque and romantic Catholic resistance against psychoanalysis (and political modernity at large) had more to do with the pleasure principle acted out in the stories of Prometheus, Narcissus, and Icarus than with Moses's Judaism.[64] The political totem was also an icon of both desire and image, and Freud saw Judaism and psychoanalysis as opposing both. In short, psychoanalytic antifascism was as much the ideological front against fascist ideology in the present as a confrontation with a barbaric past rooted in unreason, in the incapacity to think and the drive to obey the dictum of mythical leaders. This barbaric past, like fascism, was for Freud rooted in the pleasure principle.

The weak utopian dimension in Freudian thinking is to be rooted in the future. In the book he gave to Mussolini, Freud argued: "The ideal condition of things would of course be a community of men who had subordinated their instinctual life to the dictatorship of reason. . . . But in all probability that is a Utopian expectation."[65] The choice of the word *dictatorship* may work as the proverbial Freudian slip, but as Louis Althusser would have it with respect to Gramsci, Freud speaks to the future in the present tense.[66] In other words, he had the capacity to move beyond the pleasure principle, to accept cultural frustration, and to leave the barbaric past behind. It was history and politics rather than clinical interest that confronted Freud with the experience of fascism. How can the past become the present? In *Civilization and Its Discontents* (1930), Freud had stated that it was difficult for him to represent or think about the subject position of a victim of radical violence in the past: a slave, the victim of the Inquisition, or "a Jew awaiting a pogrom."[67] Suddenly he became a subject in the history of persecution and he soon realized that his own fascist present time uncannily repeated the past. The uncanny nature of fascism—its strange familiarity as a repressed content—may have reminded Freud of the unchecked violence that Jews had suffered in the past and the need to resist it.[68] This inability of modern society to accept frustration led to the dialectical return in the present of the heroic primordial father of the past. Fascism then constituted a structural repetition across time and national borders.

Fascism, the Pleasure Principle, and How Mussolini Became a "Hero"

The personal connections between fascism and psychoanalysis began not only in a simple therapeutic way but as a historical challenge to the fascist ideological emphasis on the singularity of its own myths. Was Mussolini another historical case? What was the relationship between Mussolini, the subject of Freud's dedication, and the myth that formed Freud's analogical frame of reference? Mussolini the patient was "treated" with a highly sophisticated irony that encrypted him as a radical subject for the psychoanalytic couch. But for Freud, Mussolini was not a "normal" neurotic patient but a historical one and a "hero." But what kind of hero?

One year before his visit to Freud, Forzano had coauthored a play in three acts. The subject had been Napoleon and the coauthor was Mussolini. Forzano gave this book to Freud and he wrote a dedication in the name of both authors. It read, "to Sigmund Freud who will make the world a better place, with admiration and gratitude. Benito Mussolini and G. Forzano."[69]

Thus, Freud was informed of Forzano and Mussolini's play on Napoleon and, more generally, about the Duce's tendency to think of himself as a heroic figure rooted both in political myths and in the history of leadership. Mussolini often considered himself a new Bonaparte and a new Caesar. As we have seen, Bonaparte had been a figure of central importance to Freud as well. Freud had regarded the Corsican as the leader who in historical times had returned politics to the figure of the primordial father.[70] But Freud did not want to tell Mussolini that he was Bonaparte. Besides, Mussolini would have taken this characterization as a clear compliment. The generic idea of a cultural hero was more cryptic and messier, but it equally conveyed a reading of the fascist unconscious that was certainly more complex than more standard antifascist notions of fascism such as Caesarism or Bonapartism.

Whereas Mussolini saw fascism as a sign of the future, Freud saw it as a symbol of the past. To be sure, Freud, as we have seen, often considered fascism to be rooted in the "Middle Ages." However, fascism equally implied for Freud a return to the issue of primal history, that is, the origins of human culture as he had earlier explored the subject in *Totem and Taboo* and much later in 1930 in *Civilization and Its Discontents*. In other words, Freud saw fascism as the return of the repressed, more precisely as the primacy of death over life. For Freud, the fight against fascism represented the "eternal struggle between the trends of love and death." Freud was pessimistic, as he wrote in 1931, regarding who would win.[71] For Freud, fascism projected to the political realm the most destructive instinctual forces of the unconscious.

As Giacomo Contri reminds us, some months before Freud described Mussolini as a cultural hero, Freud had written a now forgotten text in which he presented Prometheus, the fire bringer, as a *Kulturheros*, the hero of civilization.[72] Freud presented this myth as a very "obscure" one. Prometheus, according to Freud, had renounced instinctual forces by controlling them. Ironically, this act of control dialectically led to a violent return of negative instinctual forces. Controlling fire meant, at least in the short term, the possibility of human propagation of destructive fires. In Greek mythology, the heroic actions of Prometheus led Zeus to argue that as punishment for bringing fire to humans, he would make sure the former and the latter would live forever in misery.

Freud stated, "we are aware that the demand for renunciation of instinct, and its enforcement, call forth hostility and aggressive impulses, which only in a later phase of psychical development become transformed into a sense of guilt."[73] In the Greek myth, Prometheus was punished because of his act of defiance against the Gods. Civilization did not develop peacefully but rather through an action involving the violent transgression of norms. By not respecting rules (by the act of theft), Prometheus undermined the legitimacy of civilization while also making it possible. Thus, civilization relies on a delicate balance according to Freud. Like Kafka's narratives, civilization is constantly obscuring and revoking itself. Kafka, as Adorno suggests, imagined Prometheus as finally merging with the rock to which he was chained.[74] In a sense, then, Prometheus's worst fate was to be forgotten. Freud tried, by contrast, to remember the hero by unchaining him and recommending him to Mussolini, thus returning the story of Prometheus to conscious political life. Mussolini then became an unbound Prometheus, a fire bringer that was going to be punished, or so Freud may have hoped.

Six years before the Mussolini dedication, Freud opposed extreme individualism to civilization and implicitly equated the figure of the "dictator" with the persona of a narcissist who, having seized all the means to power, then rejects civilization and, with it, the Freudian need to renounce instinctual forces. The modern dictator is anachronistic; he signifies the return of the primal father who ruled the "hordes."[75]

Freud was influenced by Karl Abraham's earlier essay on Prometheus, which was published in *Dreams and Myths: A Study in Race Psychology* (1913). For Abraham the myth of Prometheus was transhistorical, presenting different configurations in different times, nations, and cultures. Like Abraham, Freud described the hero as the "creator of man."[76] Prometheus, as a hero, became the metaphor for the primal father that, in his essay on "Group Psychology," Freud presented as the original form of human authority. He described this leader as the " 'superman' whom Nietzsche only expected from the future."[77] Unlike the German philosopher, Freud valued this superman for his historical contribution and not as a source and motif of future transcendence. For him, civilization was born not from the head of the superhero but when the superhero was killed by the group. Only then did norms (the Law) become detached from the will and fantasies of the hero. In other words, only after the hero was punished did society give itself the Law according to Freud. In a new modern dialectic, the process of democratic will formation, which brought emancipation to Jews like Freud, was now threatened from within.[78]

By ending the law, the dictator becomes the law and this implies a reversal of the prenormative epoch of the primal father. This fits Mussolini's rule. In Freud's analogy between Mussolini and Prometheus, Freud may have wished to Mussolini, in implicit antifascist terms, the terrible and interminable destiny that the Gods ascribed to Prometheus. Both "heroes" shared fantasies of total mastery. But more importantly, Freud, with his usual multilayered writing style, ascribed to Mussolini, the new hero, the innate characteristics of "primitive man" and "primitive ancestors." Later on, in his book on Moses, Freud would describe the hero as an object of massive political appeal, "We know that the great majority of people have a strong need for authority which they can admire, to which they can submit, and which dominates and even ill-treats them. We have learned from the psychology of the individual whence comes this need of the masses. It is the longing for the father that lives in each of us from his childhood days, for the same father whom the hero of legend boasts of having overcome."[79] This line of thought from *Moses and Monotheism* (1939) was written under the spell of a menacing fascist context that eventually led him to exile.[80] In 1933 the Austrian dictator Engelbert Dollfuss dissolved parliament and inaugurated a regime that Freud had called a "moderate fascism." In a letter Freud made clear that he could tolerate Austrian fascism better than "detested" communism. However, with Hitler's fascism, the situation would be different. He wrote to his son Ernest: "Either an Austrian fascism or the swastika. In the latter case, we should have to go."[81]

During the Austrian crisis of 1934, when the Austrian Nazis threatened the life of incipient Austro-fascism, Freud, probably referring to Mussolini, stated: "rumor has it that a certain powerful man insisted on putting an end to the conflict which has been smoldering for long. At some time this was bound to happen." Freud was not happy that a "powerful man" was the guarantor of a dictatorial order. In short, he had to rely on a hero, Mussolini, and his allies, the Austrian fascists. They stood between Freud and his fellow Austrian Jews and the "Nazi scoundrels." It was indeed a double bind that Freud resolved by privately preferring the lesser fascist evil, namely, Mussolini and the Austrian fascists. In describing them as "the heroes and the saviors of sacred order," Freud was indisputably expressing a bitter irony, as he may have been in his dedication in 1933 to the Duce.[82]

Freud's condensed irony reflects not only his dependence but the fascist connection with the primordial hero. For him, the myth of the hero is a "lie,"[83] the first of a series that includes religion and the mythmaking that went into fascism. The leader personifies this mythmaking, these lies, this theft, and other intrigues. Freud described the historical context of global fascism as the dominium of "lies," stealing, and deceit. Fascist lies were overpowering: "The political situation. . . . It seems to me that not even in the War did lies and empty phrases dominate the scenes as they do know." Freud had the opportunity to see Nazi corruption at his home, when a gang from the SA had forced their way into the dining room. Mrs. Freud, fetching the household money, put it at the table, ironically telling the Nazis: "Won't the gentlemen help themselves?" In addition, Anna Freud gave them the money from the safe. They took $840 and Freud later observed that "he had never been paid so much for a single visit."[84]

Mussolini as a "hero" became a contextual symptom and in private Freud would define the Duce and Hitler as an "intriguer" and a "thief."[85] According to the Freudian dialectics of life and death, these characteristics follow the principles of destruction. But can fascist destruction lead to self-destruction?

Freud, like many other antifascists, wished for an internal self-destructive impulse in which Nazis would fight with one another and kill themselves. But for Freud fascist self-destruction was rooted in the fascist reification of desire, namely, a process that often reached what the historian Dominick LaCapra has analyzed as a "negative sublime" with respect to the victimization of the abjected Other.[86] Or to put it differently, he saw fascism as a psychotic ideology that in its circular search for full ideological wish fulfillment did not consider the external risks that the radical fulfillment of desire poses to the ego. In early 1933, in his essay on the question of world vision (*Weltanschauung*), Freud described two visions of the world that shared with religion the status of illusion, which "derives its strength from its readiness to fit in with our instinctual wishful impulses." Freud presented them as "phenomena which, particularly in our days, it is impossible to disregard." These were intellectual anarchism ("a derivate of political anarchism") and communism. There are many reasons to believe that, by "intellectual anarchism," Freud meant fascism. When Freud denounced the "nihilist" stress on the wishes of the unconscious that wrongly appropriated the theory of relativism for political and aesthetic purposes, he probably had in mind Mussolini's famous presentation of fascism as political relativism.[87] In this early embracement of an antifascist theory of totalitarianism, Freud opposed psychoanalysis to religion, nihilism, and communism.

I have already explained why Freud was reluctant at the time he met with Forzano to talk about fascism in explicit terms. Only later would the hidden sources of the metaphor be disclosed. In *Moses and Monotheism*, published in his short-lived exile from the fascist powers in London (1938–1939), Freud made explicit connections between fascism and communism. He nonetheless did not conflate communism and Nazism. He argued that Soviet aims were enlightened and bold, but he criticized Bolshevik means, arguing that the Soviets subjected the Russian population "to the most cruel coercion and robbed them of every possibility of freedom of thought." Freud continued, "With similar brutality the Italian people are being educated to order and a sense of duty. It was a real weight off the heart to find, in the case of the German people, that retrogression into all but prehistoric barbarism can come to pass independently of any progressive idea."[88] This retrogression defines the ultimate distinction between communism and fascism. Fascism represents atavistic forms of desire in politics, the return of the father, whereas communism represents both an idea of the future and the return of the band of brothers that had killed the father.[89] It is highly symptomatic that, in the same book, Freud's description of the imperviousness to logical thinking is cathected with political metaphors. Let me quote a highly condensed section:

> All these phenomena, the symptoms as well as the restrictions of personality and the lasting changes in character,. . . show a far-reaching independence of psychical process that are adapted to the demands of the real world and obey the laws of logical think-ing. They are not influenced by outer reality, or not normally so; they take no notice of real things, or the mental equivalents of these, so that they can easily come into active opposition to either. They are a state within the state, an inaccessible party, use-less for the common weal; yet they can succeed in overcoming the other, the so-called normal, component and in forcing it into their service.

Freud goes on to describe these negative reactions as a question of sovereignty: "If this happens, then the sovereignty of an inner psychical reality has been established over the reality of the outer world; the way to insanity is open."[90] The relation with fascism is implicit. In short, Freud considered fascism's irrational quality as mirroring the psychotic detachment of individuals, namely, as a collective rejection of reality, a complete identification with lies, and as an expression of the death drive. And he thought that self-destruction was a typical outcome for an ideology so deeply rooted in both. He was not wrong in the long term. Hitler and Mussolini finally engaged in a war that destroyed their lives, their regimes, and their countries in a final twilight of the self-prescribed heroes, a fascist *Götterdämmerung*. As we will see, Borges would also write about how fascism ends and the connections of this ending with the mythical motif of the fall of the Gods. But unlike Borges, Freud did not live to see this and wrongly identi-fied fascist self-destruction—or the primacy of the death drive that ultimately destroys the life of the ego—with the fascist purges of the 1930s. He, of course, had in mind the Nazi murderous purge of the SA in 1934—an event that he recognized as having personally enjoyed. "[Freud] told Arnold Zweig that his impression of the event presented a striking contrast to an experience he had had at the Hague Congress in 1920. There the hospitable Dutch had invited their half-starved colleagues from central Europe to a sumptuous banquet, being used to so little food they found the hors d'oeuvres a sufficient meal and could not eat more." Reflecting on this, Freud ironically argued: "Now the hors d'oeuvres in Germany leaves one hungry for more."[91]

But probably in the mid-1930s Freud could still think that Mussolini presented a moderate fascism. To be sure, Mussolini often called himself a "primitive of the future" but Freud could not risk giving Mussolini the essay on Prometheus the fire bringer that would present the Duce as the primitive of a mythical past, as the primordial boasting hero. Freud knew better. He gave him his discussion on war instead, a subject matter that, he argued, should be "a concern for statesmen." In this small book Freud strongly argued that norms were the best means to counteract the violent actions of violent individuals. The Law controls individuals and proscribes dictatorial heroic violence. Freud saw the very existence of solid norms as a barrier against fascism. And in the book, he generally criticized rulers who wanted "to go back from a dominion of law to a dominion of violence."[92] Fascism represents this primacy of violence. The message is indeed clear. Violence is politics going backward. Like classical myth, fascism, the modern form of political myth, represents the return of the past.

In Orientalist fashion, Freud does not mention Mussolini in public but refers to the Turks and the Mongols as waging wars that "have brought nothing but evil."[93] Like Voltaire or Diderot, Freud in his public statements used the Orient in order to represent the worst aspects of modern Western civilization. In private he would equate the Nazis with the "Turks" of 1683 when they "were outside Vienna."[94] The image of barbarians at the gate is hardly original but acquires specific contextual connotations. Moreover, Freud defined Mussolini and Lenin as "despots" whom he detested.[95] The idea that "Eastern" despotism is the antithesis of Western culture did not exclude, in Freud's mind, Eastern Judaism. Referring to his brother in law, he once described him as an Asiatic being in negative terms.[96] In addition, he felt the need to explain that Judaism was not "Asiatic" and thereby not fundamentally different from their European "hosts."[97]

Perhaps there is no better expression of the dialectic of the enlightenment, of its self-destructive tendencies, than the fact that Freud, the bearer of its legacy, approved its discriminatory and victimizing dimensions. He often described the Jews from the "East," presenting them as living images of physical decay and illness. Freud's family, of course, was of Eastern European origin but Freud saw himself as the Westernized counterpoint to despotic Orientalism. According to this "Orientalism," the notion of the East represents the stress on the "death drive," the sum of instinctual forces that "seek to destroy and kill." Freud could not escape some of these destructive dimensions himself. Transference played a trick on him. But all in all, Freud correctly saw that fascism meant myth, death, and violence. It expressed an unbalance in the dialectic between Eros and Thanatos, fusing ideological and aesthetic visual imperatives. In short, fascism represents the return of the repressed. The negative dialectic that Freud never made explicit is that the "repressed" is brought by modernizing forces.

The Orientalist charges notwithstanding, Freud correctly located the return of the repressed as a central part of Western history, which began with the classical hero. If Mussolini was Prometheus, he was then connected to the roots of Western civilization as Freud understood it. This was a much more important dimension in Freud's thought than the Orientalist trends that represented his own negative dialectic. The return of the repressed implies, as in the ambivalent nature of the Prometheus story, a lack of balance between negative and more positive instinctual drives rather their mutual exclusion. As he wrote in the essay he gave to Mussolini, the return of the repressed represented a pendulum between life and death that was radically inclined to death.[98] Freud could not have predicted that the Spanish fascist Millan Astray, and also the Romanian fascists, would best personify this lack of balance between Eros and Death when they chanted, "Long live Death."[99] This destructive tension between life and death was an expression of the fascist need to blur the line between the inside and the outside, that is, between instincts and the external need to repress them.

If, for Freud, civilization was born with control, repression, and limited denial of death, fascism put forward a mythological rejection of normativity and, at the same time, stressed the overdetermination of death and power. This fascist lack of balance between life and death had been previously personified in the mythical deeds of the fire bringer, that is, the provider of an element that is at the same time a metaphor for passionate love and total destruction. Freud saw Prometheus as a "criminal" and a "thief" who had been punished for breaking the norms. In bringing fire to man, Prometheus gave a "blow" to instinctual life censoring and limiting instinctual forces. These very instinctual forces that the hero suppressed lived in his inner body, that is, within himself. Tellingly for Freud, Prometheus's phoenix-like liver was the ultimate representative of instinctual forces and even a radical expression of the phallus. Thus, Freud saw the *Kulturheros* as representing both human attempts to control the instinctual drives (what Freud called "the effort to live") and their reversal in the "death instinct." The *Kulturheros* inaugurated civilization through fire but also "criminally" provided the means for civilization's own instinctual reversal or even its self-destruction. Freud saw this ambivalence of the myth in dialectic terms. This feature was central to Freud's idea of the central mythological dimension of fascism. Like Prometheus, fascism for Freud had a dual function. It could bring modernization and, in dialectic fashion, a return of the repressed. Mussolini, the *Kulturheros*, represented modernity and its dialectic outcome: unmediated violence, myth, and destruction.

{ 3 }

Borges and Fascism as Mythology

IN HIS READING OF FASCISM, Borges stressed its unconscious dimensions. Borges maintained that fascist behavior both in Europe and the Americas had to be explained, or as he put it "reasoned," by focusing on this "deepness." In 1944, he rhetorically asked: "has not Freud reasoned, and Walt Whitman intuited, that men do not have sufficient information about the deep motivations behind their behavior?"[1]

Like Freud, Borges linked the unconscious with the return of the historically repressed, that is, with mythical formations repressed at a primitive stage of the development of civilization, at a precultural stage. He thus argued in 1944 that fascism was "playing the game of energetic barbarism."[2] If one considers the occasional diatribes against psychoanalysis that were proposed by an increasingly conservative and even authoritarian Borges—especially after the fall of Peronism in 1955 when he placed himself at the antipodes of his earlier antifascist positions[3]—it is striking that in his essay of 1944 he opposed the act of reasoning of psychoanalysis to fascist barbarism.

Borges approached fascism with deep irony, but he also regarded it as a source of rhetorical and conceptual wonder. By the end of

World War II, Borges is shocked by the enthusiasm displayed by Argentina's fascists even as they sensed that Nazism's defeat was imminent. He explains this fascist mental state as a form of suspension of disbelief. In literature, the suspension of the reader's disbelief allows the story to proceed; in fascism, the suspension of disbelief becomes a wellspring of politics—it replaces the real world with ideology. It transforms the truth into lies. "The enigmatic and notorious enthusiasm of many followers of Hitler" is explained by the fact that "they have lost all notion that incoherence needs to be justified."[4] In short, Borges rejects, as he had already done as early as 1940, the possibility of rational dialogue with fascism.[5] However, unlike the typical antifascist dismissal of fascism as simply nonsensical and thus lacking any real content that can be interpreted, Borges presents the fascists as thinkers of the wrong kind.

Borges does not deny that barbarians can think, and even participate in intellectual traditions (he even makes references to barbarian reactions to Western traditions, from the Jesuitical tradition to Nietzsche), but for Borges the fascist way of thinking becomes a form of "monstrous reasoning" (*razonamiento monstruoso*).[6]

Borges understands the logic of Nazism as a deification of the "atrocious." It is an absolute rejection of normative Western ethics, in that "the end justifies the means." Borges even suggests that, for Nazism, means tend to become ends. In short, violence constitutes fascist political meaning. In a text written in 1940, he argues that Argentine fascists admire Hitler "not despite lightening bombs and fulminous invasions, machine guns, denunciations and perjuries, but precisely because of those uses and instruments." Thus, for Borges, Nazi fascism constituted a "prodigy." "It has a moral nature, and it is almost incredible."[7]

This fascist conjunction between a "monstrous" logic of interpretation and a new normativity that is, paradoxically, based upon the constant search for anomic violence leads to the death, the "beheading," of reason. This sacrificial act epitomizes the fascist search for authenticity. It embodies a poetics of "impulsiveness" and a lack of logic. Borges simplifies this fascist rejection of reason by conflating it with Nietzschean motifs. But, at the same time, he emphasizes the complex process through which the dissolution of normativity signals the transcendental absoluteness of the Nazi revolution.[8] As he argued in 1939 in an antifascist essay, "Adolf Hitler does things à la Zarathustra, beyond good and evil."[9]

In this context, violence becomes the starting point of politics, its source of power, and its origins. In this framework, the victim—in the case of the Holocaust, the Jewish Other—is transformed, like reason itself, into a sacrificial object. This Borgean insight presents conceptual convergences with several more recent theorists, from Jacques Lacan to Giorgio Agamben.

In Lacan's work, for example, the idea of Jewish sacrifice at the hands of the Nazis was an essential part of Nazism's theory and practice. The Jew represented a "god in the dark."[10] For Agamben, the Holocaust's logic of sacrifice is carnival-like, a sort of upending of subject positions that transforms the sacrificial object into a subject of ontological knowledge.[11] I disagree. This sort of analytical narrative provides full meaning to an experience that victims were not able to understand in their own context. In fact, they could not understand it insofar as their "sacrifice" only made sense to fascists. Only fascists can explain to themselves the meaning of victimization. For nonfascists in general, and the victims in particular, the Holocaust makes no sense. Thus, in terms of historical experience, the limits of representation mark the most difficult moments of working through trauma. Interpreters who did not experience the traumatic event confront, consciously or unconsciously, a conceptualization frontier.[12]

This was the case of Borges. For him, the Holocaust embodied its own lack of substantiation. It was a meaningless event from the perspective of reason. However, it was also the objective outcome of meaningful mythological formations rooted in unreason. For Borges, this rejection of reason is related to the most primal elements of fascist ideology: rational argument is replaced by images, emotions, and desires. In other words, fascism embraces imaginary politics and produces radical events that are beyond the limits of rational representation and justification.

Referring to this contextual possibility of representing horror, George Steiner emphasizes the centrality of the victim as witness and narrator. He states that "from the vast range of literature on the Holocaust, only three or four authors have managed to reach that . . . especially Celan. Without any doubt, Primo Levi. . . . There might be half a dozen texts in which I would say this incredible audacity is justified, although, at what cost?" In the examples Steiner cites, they all paid with their lives: "Celan committed suicide. Primo Levi committed suicide. Jean Améry committed suicide; all of them commit suicide long after the events, as if having been a witness of such horror would have stripped their lives, and the language they used, of all meaning."[13] They all were victims, but Borges was not. But Borges shared with them the notion that the trauma of fascist victimization transcended the actuality of experience to become the source of its interpretation.

In the cases of Celan, Levi, and Améry, the memory of horror, the act of its remembrance, provokes the end of the narrator. The three of them had tried to represent death and paid the same price as the Borgean bard of the story in which, at the king's request, a poet attempts several times to represent the famous battle of Clontarf. In the first telling, war metaphors abound. In the second attempt, metaphors give way to a direct, more literal form of representation. Here the reality effect created by the poet in his performance is almost total. In the third representation, the depiction of the battle is absolute; the poet reaches the essence of war. War is not only represented but also experienced in the poet's narrative. The poet commits suicide after achieving this representation. Ultimately by representing the unrepresentable, the narrative transcends the comprehension obtained through this representation. Then his life loses all meaning. The achievement of representing the limits eventually imposes the dissolution of all senses in death. This is presented as a mythical situation; representation becomes the myth of its impossibility.[14]

Unlike the victims of the Holocaust, the Borgean poet tries to create a story that represents but also values the violence of war. It is even possible to think of his death as a Borgean recognition of the impossibility of giving violence a normative framework. The poet tries and fails to celebrate the sovereign through a mythical chronicle of violence. He wants the myth of the sovereign to be a political theology, but he fails to represent myth outside of itself and the realm of its believers. For Borges, literature cannot provide political cover for violence, or at least cannot properly represent it in literary terms. Politics as mythology cannot be poetic. In Borges's analysis of Argentine populism this irruption of the political faith creates what Borges called a "gross mythology." Borges adopts the same perspective to think about fascism. As in the Borgean story "Ragnarök," the "heroes" of fascism no longer have a status of heroic legitimacy.[15]

The impossibility of representation is equal to the violent effects that those false idols motivate. Their violent actions presupposed, as we will see in the case of the Borgean Nazi Zur Linde, the destruction of the world as we know it and also of literature.

The modern mythology of totalitarianism, as Borges understands it, creates an "unreal epoch." In his perception of the mythical, Borges separates classical myths and modern myths. Classical myth enriches literature and, even as Borges would say in the case of the impossible hero of Cervantes, criticizes it from the domain of unreality itself. The modern myth of the hero confuses literature with violence. So for Borges, myth can represent a genealogy of literature, but also its end.

If in its classic form myth can represent the poetic, in its fascist version this mythical search of the poetic results in extreme trauma and therefore in the impossibility of its ultimate representation. In other words, it is specially the case with modern political myth that it cannot be understood outside of the faith involved and promoted by its mythological framework. Even when Nazism presents itself "as impulsive and illogical," it has not yet found its poet. Poetics as mythical politics is a "vain" enterprise. More generally, the traumatic effects of political myth, and the limits of representation that these effects create, eliminate all possibility of dialogue and establish iron borders between reason and unreason. The fascist belief in dichotomies creates concrete dichotomies and makes impossible the dialogue with the fascists. Thus, with the Argentine "Hitlerista," "A discussion becomes impossible because the crimes I impute to Hitler are a form of enchantment and merit for him." For Borges the fascists are "secret worshipers" of "cruelty."[16]

Myth and Its Limits

The limits of representation of myth can present two significant dimensions. The first is the mythical framework that prevents nonbelievers from establishing a dialogue without questioning the causes of worship, the faith and enchantment underling the myth. The second is the extreme sense of its traumatic effects and the near impossibility of representing them.

Certain representations of the victims, perpetrators, and observers could help to move these limits outward so that we can conceptualize what was previously beyond the frontier of critical theory and in sort of mythical territory. They present the historian with new possibilities of critically oriented analytic action aimed at thinking the particular language in which fascism seems to express itself. In a metaphorical sense, this is also true for certain canonical texts that preceded the ultimate outcome of fascism that is Auschwitz. For Borges, these included the works of Franz Kafka (1883–1924) and Argentina's most famous writer at the time, Domingo Faustino Sarmiento (1811–1888). As Saul Friedlander reminds us, in Kafka one finds an especially insightful presentation of the inability of individuals who stand at the margins of society to find meaning in their own victimization.

This language, this particular idiom, is constitutive of the message carried by the Shoah's most incisive narrators—Elie Wiesel (1928–2016) and Primo Levi (1919–1987), for example—in the same way as Kafka's messenger, who famously does not know what the message really means. As Wiesel argues, survivors are Kafkian messengers that cannot deliver their message, which consists of a story that cannot be told.[17]

Borges is connected to Kafka's narrative by intimate affinities, which seem to represent certain extreme situations in terms of that Kafkaesque message. In sum, both Kafka and Borges seek to narrate the unstable reality of trauma from the traumatized story of victims. In "The Metamorphosis"—I am using here Borges's putative translation of the story of 1938[18]—Gregor Samsa is aware of the gradual loss of his humanity, of the dissolution of the "self" that later would be experienced by Jews in Auschwitz;[19] in this narrative the experience of victimization finds its perfect literary analogy. Gregor can notice *the how* of this process, but the answers to *the whys* do not appear, and then, like Primo Levi, he stops asking.[20] Gregor considers the necessity of disappearing or giving his word to the shadows, as Paul Celan (1920–1970) wrote shortly before throwing himself to the water of the Seine. The same as Celan, Levi, and others, Gregor convinces himself of the need for his own disappearance.[21]

Disappearance is the synonym of a death that seems to be decided by the upper/official structures. This escapes the victims' comprehension. In this sense, it is important to note the similarity of "The Metamorphosis" to a terrifying text written by Petr Fischl (1929–1944), who would die in Auschwitz. This text, conceived in the ghetto of Terezin, presents no metaphors. Their absence introduces the reader to the world of the Shoah. The young author literally explains this process in which the loss of humanity is accompanied by the habituation to the death monologue imposed by the Nazis. Death becomes the habitus.[22]

In "The Metamorphosis," Gregor cannot even shake off the apple that his father throws at him as a bystander who cannot recognize his relative, friend, or neighbor. Confirming his self-alienation, the father does not hesitate to punish his son, that insect facing his eyes. The life in the house remains the same. The insect's room, read in hindsight, presents itself as a metaphor of the concentration camp. It is a different world for the Other that exists in the normality of the household. In this way, "The Metamorphosis" fully illustrates the situation described by Norbert Elias: the singular experience of a minority group that is stigmatized as outsider and that, at the same time, feels completely integrated ("established") in the cultural current and the political and social destiny of the majority who stigmatizes it.[23]

More contextually, for Borges and some of his contemporaries in Argentina and elsewhere, the work of Kafka provided metaphors for conceptualizing fascism and the Holocaust at the time it was taking place. Famously, in *The Trial*, a victim is killed and dies with his throat sliced "like a dog."[24] When he reflected on *The Trial* in 1937, Borges probably took notice of this execution, inasmuch as it echoed specific practices important in the Argentine context. *Degüello* (execution by cutting the throat) was the method of killing infamously used by the followers of the nineteenth-century Argentine dictator Juan Manuel de Rosas (1793–1877). Borges established comparisons between *degüello* and Hitler.[25] Although, by the beginning of the 1930s, Argentine fascists had embraced Rosas, the violence of his rule had long been denounced as "barbaric," and for Argentine liberals he was the archetype of the bad ruler. Here the work of the liberal writer and politician Sarmiento is especially important.[26] Sarmiento served as president of Argentina from 1868 to 1874, and he left a lasting imprint on the country thanks to policies such as his education reform, which emphasized a public secular curriculum. He was also a prolific writer who did much to conceptualize and popularize liberalism in Latin America. He established clear distinctions between liberalism and other political movements, such as the authoritarianism and political violence that typified episodes like the Rosas regime. Borges and Sarmiento both viewed Argentine politics through the lens of Western political philosophy. This is what led Borges to discern in global fascism elements of Argentine and Latin American notions of the modern.

But unlike Sarmiento, Borges sought to analyze the intellectual logic of unreason. In other words, he was interested in the process according to which fascism became part of a bureaucratic logic that had not existed at the times of Rosas and Sarmiento. In this sense, Kafka acted for him as a more nuanced complement to Sarmiento, a foundational (in Doris Sommer's sense) narrator of Argentine (and Latin American) literature.[27] For Sarmiento, Latin American politics was a contest between civilization and barbarism. With this frame of reference, Borges found it essential, as an Argentine writer, to evaluate fascism.

Borges postulated the possibility that there are reasons for the victim's stigmatization, but that these reasons are not evident from the perspective of the victims. In Borges's view, Kafka opened paths that allow us to understand and to pursue our own problems in conceptualizing the otherness of victimization. The relation between torment and the uncanny represents an obsessive search to find the meaning behind the context. As Beatriz Sarlo cogently notes, Borges saw in Kafkian bureaucratic depictions a process whereby the oxymoron becomes the matrix of a manifestly totalitarian social structure. This allusion is slightly masked in "The Lottery in Babylon," the Borges story published in the Argentine magazine *Sur* in 1941:

> In many cases the knowledge that certain happinesses were the simple product of chance would have diminished their virtue. To avoid that obstacle, the *agents of the Company* made use of the power of suggestion and magic. Their steps, their maneuverings, were secret. To find out about the intimate hopes and terrors of each individual, they had astrologists and spies. There were certain stone lions, there was a sacred latrine called *Qaphqa*.[28]

Here "the Company" fills the empty spaces of meaning with an ideology that produces something new, magical, and suggestive. But this gift presents a dimension of meaning located beyond reason. It is a gift of death. This is, in short, the oxymoronic moment of fascist mythology. The reference to Kafka as a sacred latrine emphasizes this contradiction.[29] The world is turned upside down, which for the elitist Borges marked the populist opening for unmediated mythical violence, which also stands for the uncannily sinister. I would argue that it is this relation between the unconscious and the violence involved in the traumatic that makes explicit the Borgean reading of fascism and the Shoah. It is a trauma that can be the subject of a reasoned explanation. And at the same time the unreason of Nazism can be explained not through reason but through its appeal to instinctual forces of barbarism. As Borges pointed out in 1944, the thinking "ego" would never be able to accept the triumph of fascism.[30]

In 1939, in an antifascist piece titled "Essay on Impartiality," Borges presented the ideological triumph of Nazism as the outcome of an incapacity to think. Rhetorical imagery replaced analytic reflexivity. He argued that this situation affected not only fascists but also many antifascists. That the fascist victory in war was a reflection of the fascist refusal of reason was predictable.

That it equally reflected antifascism's approach to reason was more unexpected and, for Borges, unacceptable: "Exclamations have usurped the function of reasoned thoughts; it is true that the foolish people who absentmindedly emit those interjections give them a discursive air, and that this tenuous syntactic simulacrum satisfies and persuades those who listen to them. The same person who swears that the war is a sort of liberal *jihad* against dictatorships soon thereafter wants Mussolini to fight Hitler: this action would annihilate his hypothesis."[31]

For Borges, there was almost no distinction between fascism and Nazism. Both embodied the "sacred" fascist attack against secular reason. Furthermore, both were essentially based on nationalism. Borges viewed any kind of nationalism as being opposed to secular liberalism. In contrast, what he called the "liberal *jihad*" replaced secular reason with a pseudoreligious take on liberalism. It claimed nationalism to be an essential attribute of democracy. It thus presented nationalism as essentially opposed to fascism. Borges criticized this sort of antifascist nationalism, with its tendency to stress national exceptionalism over secular cosmopolitanism. In reference to a book by H. G. Wells, Borges commented: "Incredibly, Wells is not a Nazi. This is incredible because almost all his contemporaries are Nazis even when they deny it or ignore it. From 1925 onward, there has been no publicist who has not been of the opinion that the inevitable and trivial fact of having been born in a given country or belonging to a given race (or a given good mixture of races) is not a singular privilege or a sufficient talisman."[32] The magic motif, a symbol of the sacred but also a trademark of the more profane Kafkian totalitarian "Company," was, according to Borges, an attribute of a global fascism that transcended its followers and also became the language of its foes. Thus, Borges argued in a book review published in 1941 in the Argentine newspaper *La Nación* that even those "who vindicate democracy, those who believe themselves to be very different from Goebbels, use the same idiom as their enemy and urge their readers to listen to the beat of a heart attuned to the intimate commands of blood and soil."[33]

For Borges there could not be true freedom if feelings and inner urges dominated the self. Most fascists thought exactly the opposite. In fascism, feelings and desires needed to be externally projected while reason was externally repressed. The body needed to become the instrumental "expression of the spirit."[34] This was the dubious fascist sense of liberation, the intuitive liberation of inwardness through feelings and emotions.

As Alfredo Rocco stated in a seminal speech of 1925, fascism liberated individuals both politically and intellectually. Rocco argued that fascism was above everything else feeling (*sentimento*) and action. As feeling, fascism emerged from the deep instincts of the race. These instincts explained the success of fascism. By embodying them, fascism determined an "irresistible current of national will." Rocco thought that action and feelings did not deter the existence of a doctrine but actually amplified it. In this sense, he argued, *fascism was also thought* (il fascismo è pensiero) and even had "a fascist logic." If logic and thought could emanate from feeling and action, fascism then could be presented as genuinely original in its understanding of the role of reason in modern politics. Rocco rather accurately concluded that fascism then essentially presented a different understanding of the political vis-à-vis other modern ideological traditions, namely, liberalism and socialism. He argued that liberalism, democracy, and socialism had differences of "method" between one another whereas fascism's differences with them implied a "dissent of conception." Fascism's idea of liberty was radically different insofar as it liberated the individual by subordinating his will to the state. This was the fascist "conception of freedom."[35] The senses were liberated in the process of identification with the leader and his state. It was not a traditional state that subordinated individuals to the norm but a state regime, the fascist regime that gathered them under the unique will of Mussolini.[36] This was not a rational union but one based on political force fields. "Mussolini is the force." As Bottai suggested, this force of character and intellect organized a "new culture." This force created "new human values" and gave "life to a doctrine and a new faith."[37] As Asvero Gravelli put it, Mussolini's action was rooted not in dogmas or "ethical precepts" but in a "fundamental sentiment that gives life its reason for being. This sentiment is the One." Thus Gravelli eventually excluded other subjectivities from the sources of fascist political meaning-making. Only "the I that becomes the One" could be the source of fascism. He argued that humanity should be realized as a sacred totality but only by focusing on this particular heroic ego. The focus on this ego relegated the masses to a place of expectation. Only the leader would deliver them from the world of "bestial concepts shaping the absolute in the matter of our early life."[38]

The unconscious was the source not only of political legitimating but also of bestial possibilities. If fascism was in a state of becoming desire, there were different types of desires that were deemed as problematic. For example, individual desires leading to independent thought, reflexive freedom, and more generally individualism were bad. If the right politics need to be outed from the unconscious, the unconscious needed to be discriminated between natural and artificial trends. Thus, other unconscious dimensions needed to be repressed. For example, it was important to eliminate the egoism that leads individuals to privilege the self over the collective and the state. There was a never-explained relation between this innate individualism, its natural roots in the unconscious, and why they were eventually described as artificial. All in all, it was clear to fascists that liberal freedom needed to be corrected. "Collective discipline," at times a "harshly cohesive" one, needed to be employed in order for fascism to exist and function properly. As Marguerita Sarfatti, Mussolini's lover and biographer, argued, there was a physiological need to limit a wider "external manifestation" of the freedom of the individual.[39] Without the proper fascist disciplining of the self, the externalization of its freedom was potentially dangerous for fascists. Freedom needed to be restricted to a sense of "obligation" to the collective represented in the state and the leader.[40]

Paradoxically, given the fascist emphasis on relying on instinctual forces and intuitions, fascism implied a full-blown repression of the senses. How to explain this contradiction? Fascism repressed a variety of drives, from sexuality to mass consumption. As the historian Falasca Zamponi argues, even the body was repressed in the fascist search for total submission vis-à-vis the leader.[41] The fascist unconscious emphasized the need to recognize the will of the leader as a true emanation of what Freud had called the death drive. This was a desire rooted in mythical conceptions of war, heroism, and aesthetic creativity, and this key dimension of fascism was not lost on Borges.

The Loss of Reason

Borges critiqued the emphasis of both liberals and fascists on the political unconscious. He questioned their stress on the inner sources of the self and their appeal to national feelings rooted in primal drives. This is the displacement of reason by a biological/corporeal imperative. Borges's concern with the loss of reason, that is, the analytical void that Nazism instigated even among those who opposed it, signaled a continuum between his antifascist essays and his more fictional works during the 1930s and 1940s.

As Beatriz Sarlo notes, in stories such as "La muerte y la brújula" (published in *Sur* in 1942), Borges understood Nazi racism as an "ideology that despises reason."[42] Nazism's rejection of reason gave meaning to the Borgean critique. For Borges, reason was the definitive answer to fascism. In this light, it would be useful to return to a Borgean insight on the genealogy of fascism.

In 1941, reviewing what he called an "accurate" essay by Bertrand Russell, Borges proposed that intellectual history was the best tool for understanding contemporary politics. The theory of fascism ("a doctrine") gave meaning and shapes to its praxis (its application). He argued that "the true intellectual flees from contemporary debates: reality is always anachronistic."[43] For Borges, in order to understand fascism, one needed to start with its intellectual genealogy. The ideology's past explained fascist behavior in the present. In this way, the beginning of the irrational theory of politics presupposed its practice. He also argued that, when attempting to explain fascism, it was more important to examine Nazi intellectuals who were active interpreters of this genealogical ideology than to examine Hitler. The motives, the ideological readings of these intellectuals, explained Hitler. They made him possible. This forceful reduction of fascist practice to a mere derivation of ideological meaning is central to Borges. It eventually allowed him to equate fascism with the anti-Enlightenment. For Borges, and Russell, the loss of rationality and the emphasis on the inner sources of the self made it easy to simply label Nazism as barbaric and juxtapose it with a sanitized, almost mythical notion of the Enlightenment.[44]

This Borgean search for the rationale for fascism reached its full potentiality in "Deutsches Requiem." Published in 1946, this story presents a Nazi narrator, Otto Dietrich Zur Linde, who reflects on the Holocaust and Nazism. Facing justice, the imaginary Nazi Zur Linde argues: "I will be executed as torturer and murderer. The tribunal acted justly; from the start I declared myself guilty. Tomorrow, when the prison clock strikes nine, I will have entered into death's realm."[45]

Zur Linde is a German intellectual who declares his admiration for Nietzsche and Spengler.[46] He debates with the latter in his essay "Abrechnung mit Spengler." Nonetheless, he unambiguously admires Spengler's military "radical German spirit." The mention of Spengler is not fortuitous. In the sentence that directly follows Zur Linde's "settling with Spengler," he states: "In 1929 I entered the Party." This apparent non sequitur makes sense in terms of the formalistic logic of Nazi ideology. In this sense, Borges is interested in tracing the direct intellectual links between the philosophical rejection of the enlightenment and its praxis in fascism. Zur Linde's conversion to fascism does not come easily: "I do not lack courage, I am repelled by violence. I understood, however, that we were on the verge of a new era, and that this era, comparable to the initial epochs of Islam and Christianity, demanded a new kind of man. Individually my comrades were disgusting to me; in vain did I try to reason that we had to suppress our individuality for the lofty purpose that brought us together."[47]

Zur Linde links this attempt to suppress the humanity of the self with the need to eliminate the Jewish Other. This ideological meaning of a new epoch—an epoch that in a sense was not to be lived by its perpetrators—was included in the Kafkian message. Celan expressed it in his poem about the "Meister aus Deutschland" who, for Celan, was a representation of death personified as a Nazi. Nazis were rather the political embodiment of unreason. Zur Linde can be equally seen as the Borgean interpretation of the Nazi attempt to turn death itself into an ideological artifact. In 1941 Zur Linde is named deputy commander of Tarnowitz, a concentration camp. He tells us that he felt no gratification occupying this position. Zur Linde adopts a Nietzschean notion of mercy. "Essentially," he says, "Nazism is an act of morality, a purging of corrupted humanity, to dress it anew. This transformation is common in battle, amid the clamor of the captains and the shouting; such is not the case in a wretched cell." This monstrous morality that fascism engenders is tested against the last sin of Zarathustra. Zur Linde states: "I almost committed it (I confess) when they sent us the eminent poet David Jerusalem from Breslau."[48]

In a significant essay written in 1938, Borges argued that in following Hitler, the Germans were "willing to sacrifice their culture, their past, their probity."[49] The poet Jerusalem represents this past and this culture. It is this part of Zur Linde's persona, his *Bildung*—his traditional German education—that he seeks to sacrifice.[50] Note that in Borges's narrative the quasi-sacrificial aspects of Nazi ideology and practice are depicted as the return of the German people to barbarism. For Borges, Nazi barbarism centered on a collective offering to the Führer.

Dominick LaCapra analyzes this essential aspect of the Nazi (and fascist) processes of victimization. He argues that sacrifice maintains an extra-moral ambivalence situated "beyond good an evil": "Indeed, it compounds ambivalence insofar as it identifies the victim with a *gift* to a divinity or divine-like being (a status Hitler held for his committed followers). Moreover, in Nazi ideology and practice certain victims were abusively debased or abjected such that the ambivalent reaction toward them, which in other contexts might even involve identification with the victim, might be resolved in a predominantly, if not exclusively, negative direction with attraction or identification being foreclosed or repressed."[51]

Zur Linde's feelings toward David Jerusalem are deeply ambivalent in the sense signaled by LaCapra. The poet's fame foreshadowed the possibility that he would have to die on the altar of fascist ideology. His death confirms what the ideology says about him. Jerusalem represents the Other. For Zur Linde, he signifies reason; therefore, he must be expunged.

Zur Linde emphasizes that the agonizing "loss" of Jerusalem is accompanied by the agonizing loss of his own self. "I agonized with him, I died with him, and somehow I was lost with him."[52] The lost ego becomes a permanent absence, a self bereft of subjectivity. In fascism, violence turns subjects into ideological artifacts. Zur Linde feels compelled to describe how he tortured Jerusalem because it is central to his inner ideological battle as a Nazi. His own search conforms to Horkheimer and Adorno's analysis of the objectification of the subject in fascism.[53] In this context, fascism turns both the Other and the Self into objects, objects that can be neutralized and eliminated.

"I was severe with him; I permitted neither my compassion nor his glory to make me relent. I had come to understand many years before that there is nothing on Earth that does not contain the seed of a possible Hell; a face, a word, a compass, a cigarette advertisement, are capable of driving a person mad if he is unable to forget them. Would not a man who continually imagined the map of Hungary be mad?. . . 'By the end of 1942, Jerusalem had lost his reason; on March first, 1943, he managed to kill himself.' "[54] Before the loss of life, reason is lost. However, there is a limit to our own capacity to understand unreason. Borges feels that it is necessary to omit the most radical violence from his narrative. It is only through ellipsis that we can approach this violence: "I decided to apply this principle to the disciplinary regimen of our camp, and. . . ." Here the fictional editor of Zur Linde's account adds a footnote, which states: "It has been inevitable to omit a few lines here."[55] This "inevitability" is marked by editorial omniscience. Obviously Zur Linde himself had no compunctions about describing his acts of extreme violence. But the fictional editor/publisher of Zur Linde's report, a person who was not there, has reservations.

The violence of perpetrators is unbearable to bystanders. As Borges suggests, this violence cannot be acceptable to those for whom the victims still remain subjects.

{ 4 }

Borges and the Persistence
of Myth

IN HIS WRITINGS ON FASCISM, Borges thought of fascism as a myth of the subject. The fascist glorification of the self resulted in mutually inclusive acts of submission and domination. In fascism men could turn themselves into servants of an ideological machinery. The objectification of the self (the flesh of the Nazi commander Zur Linde, the alienation of his victim David Jerusalem) was a key element of the civilizational apocalypses brought by the forces of fascism. For Borges, understanding these elements led to the rehumanization of the subject. If the myth of fascism turned subject into objects that could be easily killed, it was only by understanding fascist victimization processes that the subject could be recuperated from the fascist narrative of the catastrophe. This understanding zeroed in on the experience of the victims. Borges suggested in his work that it is also through the subjective experience of victims, and not only that of perpetrators or bystanders, that we can accurately approach their traumatic histories. Suffering and the experience of torture are a central element of the narrative about fascism. It is by recovering these experiences that Borges reconstituted the subject lost in Auschwitz. Borges focused on the particular journey of victims, from their moment of shock and denial to their attempts at self-awareness and distancing from the trauma that fascist ideology engenders. In short, he explored the historical connections between fascist ideology and death.

The Identity of the Victims

Like David Jerusalem, Borges's fictional victim from Breslau, another Jew from Breslau, the sociologist Norbert Elias, has addressed the particularity of the Jewish context at the time of Nazism. His special concern is the lack of recognition by Jews of fascism's implications for them. In Borges, this issue finds expression in "The Secret Miracle" ("El milagro secreto"), a short story written by Borges in 1942 and published in *Sur* in 1943, at the height of the Holocaust. In this story the protagonist, Jaromir Hladík, is not a Nazi but a Jewish victim. As in "Deutsches Réquiem," the main character is also on the brink of execution. But unlike the Nazi Zur Linde, and like David Jerusalem, the character is a Jewish intellectual.

The rationale behind the torture and death of Hladík presents us with a suggestive metaphor of the progressive differentiation between rational means and ends in fascism. It works, in short, as an inquiry into the objectification of the subject promoted by the fascist processes of victimization. Soon after the forces of the Third Reich enter Prague, Jaromir Hladík is denounced and detained. "He was taken to an aseptic, white barracks on the opposite bank of the *Moldau*. He was unable to refute a single one of the Gestapo's charges; his mother's family name was *Jaroslavski*, he was of Jewish blood, his study on Jakob Böhme had a marked Jewish emphasis, his signature had been one more on the protest against the *Anschluss*." In addition, we learn that, in 1928, Hladík had translated the Jewish mystical work *Sefer Yetzirah* (*Book of Creation*) for a German publisher. Ironically, as in the case of Jerusalem, intellectual achievements become lethal under Nazism.

"The fulsome catalogue of the firm had exaggerated, for publicity purposes, the translator's reputation, and the catalogue had been examined by Julius Rothe, one of the officials who held Hladík's fate in his hands. There is not a person who, except in the field of his own specialization, is not credulous; two or three *adjectives* in Gothic type were enough to persuade Julius Rothe of Hladík's importance, and he ordered him sentenced to death *pour encourager les autres*."[1]

In his story "Guayaquil" (1970), Borges revisited the motif of the objectification of a victim who embraces manifold identities. In this text, a seemingly arcane discussion about the origins of Argentine history presents an excuse for two historians to debate the hermeneutics of the will.[2] Here Borges returns to the topic of Nazi victimization, anti-Semitism, and the intellectual genealogy of fascism. One of the two historians is an exiled Jewish intellectual, Eduardo Zimmermann. His interlocutor is a patrician Argentine historian who in turn describes Zimmermann as a "foreign historiographer, expelled from his country by the Third Reich and now . . . an Argentine citizen."

There are interesting parallels between Zimmermann and Hladík. Both the historian and the writer from Prague are specialists in deciphering symbols. The two of them face fascist denunciation, but unlike Hladík, Zimmermann could read fascism from the illuminating perspective of diasporic exile in Latin America.[3] In the story, Zimmermann, the naturalized Argentine Jewish citizen, identifies his Argentine-born, aristocratic, and anti-Semitic interlocutor with blood, with the experience of emotions. He contrasts these features with his own Jewish experience as an analytic reader of texts. This experience is determined by the universal features of Judaism as well as by the particularities of his subject position in exile. He ironically tells the patrician Argentine historian: "You are the authentic historian. Your people wandered the fields of America and fought the great battles while my own dark people were just emerging from the ghetto. You carry history in your blood."⁴ Zimmermann identifies his aristocratic interlocutor's "authenticity" with the ability to listen to an inner voice—the voice of nationalism. In contrast, Zimmermann equates his own historical method with the act of reading. Conceptualizing, observing, and verifying evidence are central features of Zimmermann's methodology as a historian.

All in all, the Argentine Jewish historian Zimmermann represents critical reason, but his status as a person is necessarily unstable. He is established in contemporary Argentina, but he does not have a place of reference in the past. This is a sharp contrast with his interlocutor, who asks Zimmermann:

—Are you from Prague, Dr.?
—I was from Prague—Zimmermann answered.

The lack of a relational identification with the past does not prevent this past from affecting Zimmermann in his new country. The Argentine-born historian tells us about Zimmermann's academic contributions and his proclivity to defend historical losers: "From his works (without a doubt of great value) I was only able to examine a vindication of the Semitic republic of Carthage, which posterity judges from the perspective of its enemies, the Roman historians. I also examined a sort of essay where Zimmermann argues that the government should not be a visible and pathetic function."⁵

Zimmermann's liberalism is diametrically opposed to fascist totalitarian views of the state. But, more importantly, his subjective identity formation as a Jewish intellectual guarantees the same Nazi reception of his work as was the case with Jaromir Hladík in "The Secret Miracle."

Later in "Guayaquil" we read: "This argument met the decisive refutation of Martin Heidegger. Heidegger showed, through photocopies of newspaper headlines, that the modern head of state, far from being anonymous, is the protagonist, . . . the dancing David that pampers the drama of his people. . . . Heidegger also proved that Zimmermann's lineage was Hebraic, or better put, Jewish. This publication by the venerated existentialist was the immediate cause of our guest's exodus and nomadic activities."[6]

A particular adjective is what objectifies the identity of the victim, as the perpetrators (from the Nazi Martin Heidegger to the Nazi Julius Rothe) understand it. This adjective also defines Nazi fascist ideology insofar as it represents its conceived antithesis: the Jew. For the Nazis, Judaism is an identity that cannot be substantiated or denied with empirical knowledge. Rather, it is an a priori fact of totalitarian ideology.

Borges himself was accused of being a Jew by the Argentine fascist newspaper *Crisol*. Borges sarcastically responded that he accepted the charges. By occupying the place of the victim, Borges explored the experience of the Other in Argentine society, but only up to a point. There was an objective ethnic boundary that he explicitly demarcated. His ludic response to the newspaper did not transcend literary experimentation. Borges made clear to his readers that he was not actually Jewish.

> Who has not, at some point, played the game of the ancestors, the game of the prehistories of his flesh and blood? I do this often, and many times I was not repelled by the possibility of thinking myself as Jewish. This is a lazy hypothesis; it is a sedentary and frugal adventure that harms no one—it does not even damage the reputation of Israel because my Judaism was without words, like the songs of Mendelssohn.[7]

For Borges, being Jewish was a matter of hope, and from this vantage point he refuted his anti-Semitic critics: "*Crisol*, in its edition of January 30, wanted to flatter that retrospective hope of mine [of being Jewish]. *Crisol* talks about my 'maliciously hidden Jewish origins' (the participle and the adverb amaze me)."[8]

This appropriation of the identity of the victim was ambivalent. Borges believed it necessary to clarify that, contrary to Hladík or Zimmermann, the Borges family was of true Spanish background and that his anti-Semitic critics were simply wrong.[9]

Borges did not really establish a dialogue with a mythology for fascist consumption, but he contested its assumptions with an imagined historical genealogy and his own fantasies and ludic mythologies. He did not believe that the collapsing of identities was exclusive to fascism. In fact, he often described his own trajectory as that of a creator of cosmopolitan mythologies, including his own playful self-ascription of Jewish identity. However, he clearly established a dichotomy between imagined liberal mythologies, artificially conceived and carefully articulated, and the fascist mythological moment of a mere return to barbarism. Fascism denies the demands of the present and embraces the manipulation of a malleable past: "Like the Druses, like the moon, like death, like next week, the remote past is one of those things that ignorance can feed from."[10]

For Borges, the fascist enactment of mythology was founded in a political longing for this "remote past," and as such this past "is endlessly plastic and pleasant. It is much more obliging than the future and it demands less efforts. It is the favorite station for mythologies."[11]

In contesting fascist mythical notions of the past, Borges understandably tended to emphasize the global contextual trends shared by victims and victimizers but, at the same time, he was prone to collapse contextual differences and distinctions between them. In fact, for Borges, Judaism was a universal entity. Judaism, like Kafka, lacked, in his view, any particularity.[12] Borges, in general, did not distinguish between Jewishness as signifying a particular group of people (ethnic or religious) and Judaism as a universal culture. In 1941, Borges stated that this universality of Judaism was a source of personal identification and the "principal" reason "for me not to be anti-Semitic." He argued that the "difference between Jews and non-Jews seems to me, in general, insignificant; sometimes illusory or imperceptible."[13]

It is not the loss of Jewish identity as much as the loss of German cultural traditions that concerned Borges: "I am personally offended, less because of Israel and more because of Germany; less because of the insulted community and more because of the insulting nation. I am not sure that the world can exist without German civilization."[14] Moreover, his indignation regarding the loss of German identity went hand in hand with amazement. This amazement was also provoked by the gradual symbiosis between Hitler and Germany. He explained this wonder as deriving from the uncanny nature of fascism, the foreignness of Nazism vis-à-vis Germany.

Hitler became the object of Borgean hatred precisely due to his brutality and his lack of cosmopolitan German *Bildung*. As he said in 1939, "I abominate of Hitler precisely because he does not share my faith in the German people, and also because he believes that in order to get even with 1918, there is no other pedagogy than barbarism and no better stimulus than the concentration camps."[15]

Borges was less concerned with Hitler than with his intellectual followers in Europe and Latin America. He worried about those followers of fascism renouncing a culture that Hitler never had. Anti-Semitism was a practical symptom of a global ideology. Without engaging in nationalism, Borges sought to emphasize national cultural distinctions as distinctive elements of modern secular cosmopolitanism, and how these distinctions were rooted in a shared notion of modernity that actually contradicted the transnational character of fascism. He clearly recognized the Catholic self-ascription of Argentine fascist anti-Semitism, but he also noted the global connections that put its Argentine nature into question. "Certain ungrateful Catholics—that is, people affiliated with the Church of Rome, which is a dissident Israelite sect with Italian personnel, open to its customers on holidays and Sundays—want to introduce a sinister doctrine, with confessed German, Ruthenian, Russian, Valachian, and Moldovan origins."[16] Borges clearly equated anti-Semitism with a brand of Argentine right-wing Catholicism. Moreover, Borges ironically presented the "obscene word 'anti-Semitism'" as a "somber rosary" that makes "the alarmed Argentine" think about a "conspiracy."[17]

Anti-Semitism could be Argentine or German, but in Argentina it was anchored in a mistaken reading of an otherwise plural Christianity: "Those who recommend its use often blame the Jews, all of them, for the Crucifixion of Christ. They forget that their own faith has declared that the Cross made our redemption. They forget that blaming the Jews is tantamount to blaming vertebrates or mammals."[18] Beyond the irony lies the motif of universalism. For Borges this was the key feature of the Judeo-Christian dimensions of Western culture. He ironically presented Jewish universality as an emblem of the sacred. In this context, Borges demythologized the religious past as a source of contextual embarrassment and political anachronism for Argentine clerico-fascists:

> They forget that when Christ decided to be a man, he preferred to be Jewish. He did not choose to be French or even *porteño* [a citizen of Buenos Aires]. He did not choose to live in 1932 after Jesus Christ, so he could get a one-year subscription to *Le Roseau d'Or*. They forget that Jesus, certainly, was not a convert to Judaism. The basílica de Luján [a famous church in Buenos Aires Province] for him would have been a spectacle as indecipherable as a calendar, a gas heater, or an anti-Semite.[19]

In his fiction at this time, Borges depicted Catholic anti-Semites as anti-Christian. This can be seen, for example, in "Death and the Compass" (1942), in the dialogue between an anti-Semitic police inspector, Treviranus, and a Jewish journalist from a Yiddish newspaper published in Buenos Aires. Treviranus rejects history as a clue for criminal interpretation and argues: "I am a poor Christian. . . . Carry off those *musty volumes* if you want; I don't have any time to waste on Jewish superstitions." The Jewish intellectual, who, like Borges, is "myopic, atheistic and very shy," answers Treviranus that Christianity is, above all, a form of Jewish superstition.[20]

Borges contrasted universalism (as a humanistic worldview) with global or transnational anti-Semitism and fascism. For Borges, fascism was not a misguided reading of culture but a antidemocratic rejection of universal civilization. In fascism, the subjectivity of the Other is rejected and with it the possibility of an ethico-political form of self-awareness. Transnational fascism rejects reason and embraces superstition. For Argentine readers of the 1940s, the character Zur Linde synthesized two fascist national myths, the Argentine and the German fascist rejections of reason, insofar as both were under the spell of global fascism. But Zur Linde seems to acknowledge the Borgean objection to the Argentine fascist appropriation of Christianity as artificial. Zur Linde is pagan or even anti-Christian. Far from religion, Zur Linde embraces an instrumental form of victimization.

The Gaze of Trauma

In Borges, interpretative emphasis is placed less on victims than on those who inflicted the trauma. According to the Borgean gaze, the assassins participate in a process of degradation of civilization that they can only understand at the end of their lives. This belated understanding escapes their victims. Victims obviously do not choose trauma, while Zur Linde finds ideological meaning in his own death. In the Borgean narrative of Nazism, both victims and victimizers encounter death. Zur Linde is the subject of a criminal trial. The evidence against him is substantial and he does not deny it. In contrast, in Hladík's case one finds a summary trial which is explicitly Kafkian.

Terror and death are the essential dimensions of Hladík's "Trial": "Hladík's first reaction was mere terror. He felt he would not have shrunk from the gallows, the block, or the knife, but that death by a firing squad was unbearable. In vain he tried to convince himself that the plain, unvarnished fact of dying was the fearsome thing, not the attendant circumstances, senselessly trying to exhaust all their possible variations. He infinitely anticipated the process of his dying, from the sleepless dawn to the mysterious volley."[21] Here, as elsewhere in Borges, the torture suffered by the victims is contrasted to the values of reason, as Borges understands them.

This form of torture is that of Kafka's *The Trial*, in the sense that victims are unable to understand the reasons behind their victimization. In this context, death does not have a meaning. But Borges decides to move away from Kafka at the moment when God freezes time and space for Hladík, just before his execution. The divinity stops time in order for Hladík to finish the writing of his play, which is symptomatically titled *The Enemies*. In this framework death acquires a transcendental meaning and the Kafkian universe of the play becomes part of the structural sense of its author's life. Reality is thus ordered and reconstructed in the mind of the victim. In other words, it is framed as such beyond the reality principle. Zur Linde, Hladík, and David Jerusalem are embedded in the schizophrenic world of the Shoah. Living under different circumstances, the three of them are unable to deny the charges. They all accept their impending death.[22]

However, victims do not justify the destruction of their bodies. In contrast, the perpetrator Zur Linde accepts his personal defeat because he sees it as a corporeal sacrifice for something nobler than himself: "An inexorable epoch is spreading over the world. We forged it, we who are already its victim. What matters if England is the hammer and we the anvil, so long as violence reigns and not servile Christian timidity? If victory and injustice and happiness are not for Germany, let them be for other nations."[23] The principle of mythical incarnation leads to total victory or defeat. As Hannah Arendt reminded us, it was Goebbels who said in 1943: "We will go down in history as the greatest statesmen of all times or as their greatest criminals."[24] It is possible that Borges had in mind these actual words by the Nazi leader when he represented the fascist view of history not as a result of a reading of the past but as a myth of the victors. In Zur Linde's view, history is a mere artifact. The experience of the Holocaust opens up the possibility of a fascist future without the fascists that had conceived it. The myth of fascist violence remains and is now epochal. It is here to stay. Zur Linde, the leader of the concentration camp universe, now embodies the impossible fascist conflation of the biological and the political. The ideological imperative of fascism triumphs over his own body and the materiality of everything else. "I look at myself in the mirror to discover who I am, to discern how I will act in a few hours, when I am face to face with death. My flesh may be afraid; I am not."[25]

Zur Linde realizes that he has almost achieved his desire to leave behind the human in him. He no longer feels fear. The myth of fascism has finally incarnated. This lack of humanity is absolutely ideological in the fascist sense. So is the violence, insofar as terror is Nazism's final aim. "So long as violence rules" ("Lo importante es que rija la violencia"), Zur Linde declares.

The radical rupture of the "ego" (yo) that the Nazi perpetrator experiences—in other words, the total separation between, on the one hand, fear and death and, on the other hand, a Self that, losing corporeality, becomes an absolute representation of ideology—reveals an ideological world in which violent desire reigns without normative restrictions. Fascism promotes the elimination of norms and the imposition of the rule of violence. The result is an effervescence that continually acquires its own substantiation in the traumatic. It displaces the threshold of political and ethical stability through the objectification of the Other and the sacrifice of the Self.

Borges noted, however, that fascist society does not intend to be anomic. Rather, it is marked by the principle of the leader, the *Führerprinzip*. The fascist hero's desire replaces the normative legacy of the enlightenment and its values. The leader's desire becomes the law. If desire represents the only possible legality, nothing is clearly legal. This situation is symptomatic of fascism's centripetal tendency toward self-destruction. The lack of norms signals a world in which "happiness" and "injustice" go together.

For Zur Linde, the elimination of the ego even applies to Hitler himself. Hitler's "ego" is displaced by his "will and the blood."[26] Here fascism conceives the ego as providing false consciousness rather than self-understanding. In Zur Linde's testimony, the victim and death are unified by the logic of sacrifice. For Zur Linde, the victim's Holocaust is inevitable. For him it is equally inevitable that the assassin (that is, he himself) also needs to die. Thus, Zur Linde presents his own sacrificial immolation as a result of his belief in "violence and the faith of the sword."[27]

In the perpetrators' eyes, their own sacrifice makes them one with their victims. The annihilation of the ego, its loss within a moral absolute of desire, is eventually recognized as an ideological mandate that presents the gift of death as the sacrifice of the Self.[28] The new era of violence, although presented as "perfection," represents in reality a grotesque return to the repressed that, as LaCapra has stated, is a central theme in Nazism's ideology and practice.[29]

The "New Order" begins, according to Nazism, with the sacrifice, not only of the victims, but also of their victimizers. As Zur Linde states: "Let Heaven exist, even though our dwelling place is Hell" ("Que el cielo exista, aunque nuestro lugar sea el infierno").

The theme of the sacrifice of the ego for the sake of the ideology of barbarism constituted a significant yet not sufficiently recognized contribution of Borges to the theory of fascism. In an essay from 1939 Borges anticipated Zur Linde's sacrificial argument in a strikingly similar way, but he inverted the position of the subject. Borges, as bystander, would never sacrifice himself for the sake of ideology. He claimed that if he had "the honor of being German," he would never "sacrifice the intelligence and probity of my fatherland." In contrast with his imagined Nazi, Borges argues that "it is possible that a German defeat would mean the ruin of Germany; it is indisputable that a German victory would mean the ruin and the debasement of the world."[30]

Zur Linde is able to identify the indelible stigma of trauma produced by the universe of the camps. This stigma also, but not equally, prevails in the memories of the victims. Borges would later define this situation as a mark of the post-Holocaust Jewish condition. He speaks of this in the face he describes in his poem "Israel" (1969): "a face condemned to be a mask,. . . a man lapidated, burned, and drowned in lethal chambers."[31] Such is the stigma of sacrifice—it makes sense only according to the fascist logic of its perpetrators. But this ludic interplay of meaning, of interchangeable subjectivities in the mirroring images of perpetrators and victims, has its limits. For Borges the "masks" of both Zur Linde and Hladík are removed. Their search for ultimate understanding is reached through death. When Borges assumes a Jewish ego in his fiction and non-fiction and identifies with the victims, he appropriates their trauma. This ostensibly offers total understanding for the observer (or belated bystander) and readers. Yet this understanding is the outcome of a sacrificial view. Sacrifice acquires meaning in the Borgean interpretation of fascism, but at the cost of the framing of trauma, and more importantly its domestication. Trauma is domesticated as a symbol of that which Lacan analyzes as "the Real," that is, the unconscious.[32] In this framework, trauma becomes a metaphor of the fascist unconscious, of a totalitarian ideology that, like Zur Linde, rejects critical reason.[33] The Borgean gaze, so perceptive in understanding Zur Linde (and fascism), ultimately seems to sacrifice the victims by transforming them into agents of knowledge illuminated by trauma. Hladík's success as an author, his achievement of closure, is the product of the gift of death that his murderers granted him. In this regard, even God in the story might seem to agree, or at least not disagree, with the Nazis.

Hladík understands, and of course despises, the insanity of Nazism, but the effects of this ideology give him meaning as a Jewish antifascist writer and intellectual. Moreover, it would seem that, in Borges, Nazism gives the victims the possibility of writing under the effects of trauma. These traumatic charges illuminate their analytical skill and provide them with the will to "redeem" themselves: "He [Hladík] felt that the plot I have just sketched was best contrived to cover up his defects and point up his abilities and held the possibility of allowing him to redeem (symbolically) the meaning of his life."[34] However, in a typical Borgean operation, after the achievement of understanding, the symptoms of madness and death return. It cannot be otherwise. Borges emphasizes the centrality of the calculating methods of Nazi victimization. They serve an ideology rooted in the instinctual forces of desire and barbarism. Victims can search for and achieve meaning, but they can never understand fascist ideology. In Borges, their illumination is transitory. It is almost an illusion. After understanding, Hladík is restored to his previous state of numbness. Hladík returns to the lived trauma to again be drowned in its midst. The return of his senses restores him to reality. In this context, he is a lost victim: "He concluded his drama. He had only the problem of a single phrase. He found it. The drop of water slid down his cheek. He opened his mouth in a maddened cry, moved his face, dropped under the quadruple blast. Jaromir Hladík died on March 29, at 9:02 A.M."[35]

One might argue that Hladík's understanding, his deciphering of symbols, was, in the end, a denial of his traumatic condition, but this is only one dimension of the Borgean text. The participation of the sacred seems to give meaning to a death that does not have any meaningful secular connotation. More measured, and more engaged in a sort of empathic unsettlement, the Borgean representation of the last days and hours of David Jerusalem is that of the *Musselman*. As in Primo Levi's description of them, Zur Linde prompts Jerusalem to abandon the world and its realities.[36] As in the case of the death of Doctor Marcelo Yarmolinsky, the kabbalist who is murdered in cold blood in "La Muerte y la Brújula" ("Death and the Compass," 1942), the death of Jerusalem is the outcome of a break of the normative condition. It symbolizes the return of the repressed, the past, life, and, above all, death, "the secret morphology of the evil series" (la "secreta morfología de la malvada serie").[37] Borges does not attempt to understand Jerusalem and he narrates the suicide of this ghost-like figure not as a decision motivated by the reality of trauma but rather as a rejection of this reality through the recourse to madness and desperation.[38]

Jerusalem has the traumatic stigma of Auschwitz, but unlike Zur Linde, he does not understand. Only fascist ideologues understand the logic of a system of symbols that debases reason and reifies the unconscious. The inner self is presented as the bearer of a corporal mark. Jerusalem is a symbol of the trauma of reason and the regression to the repressed. He is a victim of transnational fascism. His defeat is that of the civilizing process. Fascism annihilates the progressive pacification of social space. It inscribes its defeat in the bodies of the victims. In this sense, Jerusalem is given the same ideological stigma that Elie Wiesel was able to recognize as a ruptured fractioning of the self. But Wiesel is not able to understand this after his liberation when, after battling life and death for two weeks in a hospital, he looks at himself in a mirror: "I had not seen myself since the ghetto. From the depths of the mirror, a corpse gazed back at me. The look in his eyes, as they stared into mine, has never left me."[39]

{ 5 }

A Fascist History

Carl Schmitt's Political Theory of Myth

WRITING IN HIS PRIVATE DIARIES, Carl Schmitt ironically reflected on Freud's interpretation of history, religion, and myth. He presented Freud's book *Moses and Monotheism* as "a sociological film of impressive suspense."

He argued that it was "difficult to say where" the greatest sociological suspense was. He was not sure whether it was "in Moses, in the religion of Yahweh, in the myth of the devoured father, in the interpretation of Christianity, or in this author himself."[1] To be sure, Schmitt did not disagree with Freud's idea of myth as being a central element for the interpretation of history, politics, and the present, but Schmitt's own approach was diametrically opposed to Freud's in that it was a critique of myth from within.

Carl Schmitt's work defines the history and theory of political myth. But its analysis represents a challenge to historians and theorists alike.[2] For many historians, Schmitt should be, above all, understood in his own fascist or reactionary context, while for many theorists the force of his writings transcends the particular context where he conceived his ideas. Are these positions mutually exclusive? In this chapter, I argue that this does not need to be the case. Schmitt not only contributed to the fascist theory of myth and its novel enactment as the driving force of fascism but also represents one of the most intriguing and influential interpreters of the political theory of myth. To complicate matters, Schmitt himself used history and theory interchangeably and, in fact, did not often dissociate history from the mythical.[3] His idea of history is, at times, contextually demarcated but also, at many other times, transhistorical or theological. Despite his own mythical tendencies, as a historical source and also as a theoretical auteur, Carl Schmitt needs to be put in context. In short, he needs to be returned to the era when modern ideas of political myth took shape.

If Schmitt has been so influential in more recent times (from Jürgen Habermas to Hans Blumenberg and many others), it is important to stress the fact that he was an active adversary of the most critical theories of modern political myth at the time of their inception. In redefining the role of myth against reason, Schmitt was not only a "symptom" of his times, but he became an active participant in the conceptualization of political myth in history and theory. His case shows how the myths of fascism are a key to understanding the complex genealogy of the modern political theory of myth.

Schmitt Between History and Theory

History was central to Schmitt. Many of his most relevant works can be presented as conceptual histories of politics as well as explorations of changes over time regarding historical paradigms as well as legal and theological conceptions of order and space. Unsurprisingly, Schmitt tended to strictly separate historiography from the interpretation of history. Like many other theorists, then and now, Schmitt clearly relegated the former to issues of methodology or description while he cautiously identified his approach with the latter. Was Schmitt a historian? Certainly he was not one in terms of the modern rules of the field. It would be hard to consider Schmitt a colleague if we accept Reinhart Koselleck's notion of the emergence of modern time as the moment when history "gained a genuine historical meaning, distinct from mythical, theological or natural chronological origins."[4] Mythical and divine foundations were central to Schmitt's approach to history, as he often repeated in his conversations with historians. Ironically, Koselleck, the historian, was a disciple of Schmitt, the political mythologist.[5] Both authors shared a profound interest in the great parallelisms that existed between historical epochs and how their reformulation at different contexts changed different epochal ways to think about history. More specifically, both Schmitt and Koselleck were interested in how mythical investments operated in the perception of time and also in politics. Both master and disciple shared an indictment of enlightened modernity, which they saw as putting into question the sovereign autonomy of the political.[6] They put forward a view that repositions the place of the sacred in modern history. But if Koselleck was more exclusively interested in these histories of meaning-making to rethink the assumptions of modern historiography, Schmitt presented a model of politics that heavily relied on theology and myths. Finally, if for Koselleck, and for that matter all other disciplinary historians, myths cannot transcend their metaphorical or symptomatic nature, for Schmitt myths dually became a form of representation as well as real existing things. His self-regard as a Catholic thinker was one of the reasons for this belief. As he often put it, as a Christian one had to rely on faith to think the historical. But this was not for him the only mythical way to deal with history. For Schmitt, and obviously he was not alone here (enter many thinkers at the antipodes of Schmitt such as Hans Blumenberg, Walter Benjamin, José Carlos Mariátegui, and many others), myth is not only a metaphor for reality or a symptom of mental prehistorical realities (as it was, for example, in the case of Sigmund Freud, whom Schmitt explicitly criticized in terms of his approach to mythical figures such as Hamlet). Myths can become a reality and not its mere representation. Myths are central to Schmitt's irrational sense of history. *Mythos* was for him a gateway to a deeper historical understanding. With Georges Sorel, he argued that all historical developments which are transcendental are rooted in their predisposition toward the mythical. Time and place were repositories where the mythical was actualized.[7] Schmitt did not believe that "historical knowledge can replace the myth."[8] For him, myths are interrelated with history and can be used to go beyond more rational and empirical ways of understanding the past, including mythical representations from the past, or as he put it in 1942, he looked for a "step beyond the mythological into the mythical proper."[9]

Schmitt saw mythical formations as constitutive historical symptoms of the present and future of the political. Throughout his work, Schmitt intermittently considered myth and theology as being located in and out of history. For the German thinker, myths often epitomized entire eras or problems such as in the case of the myth of Hamlet, but at other times, mythical formations also stood for Schmitt's very personal notion of the transcendental in history (such as in the medieval notion of the *Katechon* or the myths of fascism). It is especially the idea of the *Katechon* that has been extremely appealing to many Schmitt's specialists. I find this appeal as being often out of context. It betrays an excessive focus on the *Katechon* as the key to understanding Schmitt in history and theory. The fixation on this obscure eschatology as a way to provide closure to Schmitt's often ambivalent, or even antithetical, notions of theology and myth contrasts with what I see as a less-integrated dimension of Schmitt's approach to the sacred and the political.

With this disproportionate focus on the myth of the *Katechon*, the context of Schmitt's often contradictory, and at times even inarticulate, approach to the mythical, the political, and the antagonistic is lost.[10] Too much has been made of relevant, if relatively scarce, references to this medieval mythical concept. To be sure, according to Reinhard Mehring, the author of the most informed biography of the German fascist jurist, Schmitt said that 1932 was the year when he formulated his notion of the *Katechon* for the first time. But most of his references to this myth are mainly from the late years of World War II when a defeat of Nazism became a possibility. For example, he mentioned the *Katechon* in *Land and See* (1942) and made other references to it in the intense early postwar period.[11] In the aftermath of the demise of Nazism, Schmitt was sporadically in prison for his Nazi activities. In this context he thought of the *Katechon* when he was finishing the manuscripts for *The Nomos of the Earth* (1950) and *Ex-Captivitate Salus* (1950). In the *Nomos*, Schmitt presented the *Katechon* as providing historical continuity and true legitimacy to medieval power: "The Christian empire was not eternal." For Schmitt its power resided in a transcendental view of history. As opposed to the replacement of piety by legal myths, the *Katechon* acted as a true faith, providing historical and spatial stability to power: "The decisive historical concept of this continuity was that of the restrainer: Katechon. 'Empire' in this sense meant the historical power to restrain the appearance of the Antichrist and the *end* of the *present eon*."[12] Schmitt associated his finding of the role of this myth with true historical understanding. He mentioned what he thought were the right sources to frame the medieval period "in terms of its concrete historical authenticity." But if pointing to the right sources to show his historiographical credentials was enough for him in the *Nomos*, in his private writings he went one step forward. Beyond signaling the functionality and metaphorical nature of myth in history, he thought that this specific myth gave history a fully transcendental value. Thus in his private diary, his *Glossarium*, Schmitt stated: "I believe in the Katechon; for me he is the sole possibility for a Christian to understand history and find it meaningful."[13]

In the introduction to the *Nomos*, Schmitt argued that he wanted to overcome an "elemental-mythological approach," which one can identify with the position he embraced in his private entries to the *Glossarium*. In fact, as reflected in his overall work, analyzing myth to explain breaks in historical paradigms of power and space was more important to Schmitt than openly stating or elaborating on his more private messianic views. Of course, if one believes that these private, or at times semiprivate, sporadic moments act as a scholarly form of revelation, it would then be tempting to think the *Katechon* as a way to downplay Schmitt's fascist views. Fascism would be a mere temporal container for the *Katechon*. But Schmitt's fascist views had nothing to do with medieval eschatology. Order and stability were key desires for Schmitt, but he was more of a counterrevolutionary than a reactionary. His antirational illiberal views were essentially modern. So was his anti-Semitism. It is true that Schmitt thought that the *Katechon*, and other myths, could be instantiated in both the state and the powerful. This is how one could read his now famous essay from 1934 on Hitler as the lawgiver. Here juridical truth was equated with the transcendental nature of the leader. Hitler famously represented himself as "the supreme judge of the Nation." Hitler was for Schmitt the embodiment of the "most authentic jurisdiction."[14] But how significant is this text?

Schmitt was not only fixated on an imaginary unitarian past as represented by Hitler's leadership. He also believed in a unitarian future. In and out of past and future, myth provided a continuum for these beliefs. When myths of literary or real figures, institutions, and nations changed, times also changed. This understanding of the role of myth in history Schmitt especially put forward in the 1920s and 1930s.

Schmitt was theoretically closer to Italian fascism than German Nazism. In fact, the racist absolutism of Alfred Rosenberg, the Major Nazi theorist of Myth, was quite removed from

Schmitt's conceptions. For Rosenberg, "The sun myth of the Aryan is not only transcendental but also a universal law of nature and biology." Rosenberg argued: "Mythic feeling and conscious perception no longer confront each other as antagonists but as allies."[15]

Whereas Rosenberg presented a transhistorical clash of racially rooted mythical traditions, Schmitt was more concerned about the ways in which mythical incarnations provided the synthesis of law and power. To be sure, Rosenberg also presented the new myth that would dominate Germany and the world as a form of embodiment of mythical racial traditions, but he was not concerned at all by legality and legitimacy.

In contrast, for Italian fascists, power as incarnated in the leader became the source of normativity. In this sense, power and desire in fascism became the law. As the reactionary Russian thinker Nicolas Berdiaeff put it, fascism was against the traditional notions of political legitimacy, the formalist legalism of rationalism. The fascist dichotomy of Law and Life rendered the former a death object. For Berdiaeff, with fascism, the principle of force displaced the juridical principles of monarchies and democracies alike. The vital energy of a collective union of social groups replaced the atomization of individualism and affirmed life.[16] Most Argentine fascists as well as many of their Spanish colleagues concurred with Berdiaeff on the medieval dimensions of fascism. But as opposed to the Italian fascists' more secular notion of the sacred as deeply rooted in the heroism of the leader, for many Argentines and Spaniards God played a central role in the Argentine and Spaniard fascist politics of self-interiorization. The leaders were also deified, but at the same time, dictators like Uriburu or Franco were presented as being recipients of God's gift.[17]

Despite these differences over the role of the sacred in their politics, fascists on both sides of the Atlantic agreed on the need for fascism to embrace the mythical through the unlimited "dominant power" of the inner self. This affirmation of power led to a new form of fascist normativity. Fascism displayed an immanent force in a state of consciousness and eventually this force became the norm.[18]

Similarly the Argentine fascist Leopoldo Lugones prophesied a new dictatorial Latin America where incarnation would be the result of the actualization of the mythical past of warriors in the political desert of the present. For Lugones this mythical incarnation was above legality, which was rendering an empty form to be filled by the new type of leaders.

In 1924, some years before Schmitt's idea of the Law as the result of Hitler's will, Lugones announced his idea that norms needed to be an expression of the will of the leader. [19]

Lugones saw this leader as the man who commands because of his right as a better. "He rules, with or without the Law. Because the Law, as an expression of potency, is fused with his will."[20] This idea of the norm as related to the segmented fascist process of mythical incarnation was more generally clear in fascist ideas of subjectivity.

Fascism always longed to return to its violence and nonrational origins. Not doing so would imply a state of decadence. However, the return to origins could not put into question the fascist institutionalization of the state. The result of this tension between political desire and the norms represented in the state was often objectified in the persona of Mussolini. He created and embodied the permanent fascist state of revolution.

The idea of the norm as a malleable expression of the I of the leader was directly linked to the fascist attempt to reconciliate the mythical inner self with the subjectified outside world. Thus, in fascism norms could not be static but rather the expression of the natural authenticity of the leader.

Like Schmitt, fascists simplified the opposition between reason and intuition as an attempt to discuss its supposed conflation by liberalism and Marxism. As Mussolini argued, *Homo economicus* did not exist: "the man that exists is the integral man, which is political, which is economic, which is religious, which is a saint, which is a warrior."[21] The idea of the integral man was driven by the fascist emphasis on denying reason and logic any place in the search for an authentic form of self-understanding. Instinctual forces were not logical or reasonable but passionate and inflexible.

Schmitt's idea of political myth was more sincerely identified in Mussolini's embodiment of living political myths than in a transhistorical Catholic medieval notion. At least before 1945, modern fascist theories of political myth were more significant for him than the *Katechon* in explaining how sovereignty could be established and affirmed.

All in all, Schmitt's references to the *Katechon* are clearly important, but it would be hard to ascribe them back to Schmitt's body of work of the interwar and Nazi years. In someone like Heinrich Meier, this totalizing ascription of the *Katechon* as the way to read Schmitt as historian and theorist becomes even more problematic, even when relegated to the postwar period. For Meier, the *Katechon* gave Schmitt "security" to "remain in harmony with himself."[22] Meier goes as far as to argue that for Schmitt medieval myths linked theory and history in such a way that they provided meaning to history and linked it back to the sacred. Thus, for him Schmitt's "consciousness of 'historicity' was rooted in the apocalyptical." This view projects Schmitt's moments of mysticism into his plural conceptions of the mythical. These views significantly changed over time. Schmitt's long-standing search for order and stability was constantly reformulated in different contexts. However, one of the things that remained present both before and after 1945 was his modern view of the role of political myths in history. This view was more Sorellian, and at times clearly fascist, than medieval. In other words, for Schmitt, myths had a revolutionary impact (or a counterrevolutionary one), as living embodiments of changes in historical structures and paradigms. Modern historicity was more significant for Schmitt than eschatology. To be sure, Schmitt never left behind the messianic dimensions of his thought. These dimensions were especially powerful in the early postwar period. But Schmitt intermittently conflated and integrated the "weak messianic" thinking that affected thinkers on the other side of the fascist/antifascist spectrum. For example, this was the case of famous antifascists thinkers like the historian Gershom Scholem, the theorist Walter Benjamin, and the Peruvian Marxist intellectual José Carlos Mariátegui. But if the former identified with a myth that recuperated the historical defeats of the victims, Schmitt clearly identified with the vanquishers.

The Myth of the Vanquishers

Schmitt identified myth with legitimacy, but, as could be expected, this identification did not separate fact from myth. This is exactly how in 1938 he addressed the ethical legacy of Hobbes at the end of his anti-Semitic book: *The Leviathan in the State Theory of Thomas Hobbes*.[23] A similar ending celebrates the fascist embracing of modern political myth in his *Crisis of Parliamentary Democracy*.[24] In other texts, Schmitt had been equally implicit about identifying the winning side of the present with fascism. In 1927 and 1929, he even mocked others for prophesying that Mussolini was going to fall.[25]

The argument of myth as a reality that linked the past, present, and future was first anticipated in Schmitt's essay "The Political Theory of Myth" of 1923, later reproduced in his book against parliamentary democracy. Here Schmitt stressed the centrality of Sorel for thinking the mythical as a construction that, on a deeper level, implied a revelation. In Schmitt, history, myth, and theory were intimately tied. As he explained in *Land and Sea* (1942), myths were repositories of the most intimate memories and experiences of the people. In and through them, people could go back to their foundations. These "deep, and at times, unconscious, memories" pointed to the "mysterious" origins of life.[26]

Here again, Schmitt shared with most fascists their idea of consciousness as a result of the outing of a fascist unconscious. For Schmitt, true historical interpretation could not exist without the act of recognition of deeper and prehistorical or transhistorical meaning. This belief is at the center of Schmitt's peculiar theory of history. This theory is as much historical as it is a theory of myth in politics. Myths had to be first identified and then glorified. This exercise implied not only a thoughtful construction but also an irrational affirmation of political energies. In Schmitt, myths and legends represented a hidden historical truth that figures, institutions, or concepts were able to make tangible. In other words, myths existed in history as a mark of true meaning. They were vital and sacred forces that explained history and transcended it. In this regard, in her illuminating book on political myth, the Philosopher Chiara Bottici observed that, in Schmitt's conception of the mythical, myth and reason are "heterogeneous and mutually irreconcilable." For her, Sorel was more rational than Schmitt. Bottici distinguishes between a Sorellian view of identification with myth as a conscious choice and Schmitt's own idea of myth as a "destiny."[27] In contrast, the political theorist, and key expert on Schmitt, Andreas Kalyvas stresses the Sorellian instrumental nature of Schmitt's conception of the mythical. While Bottici's explains how myth was for Schmitt part of a "destiny," Kalyvas stresses the modernity of Schmitt's conception of myth as being not merely prepolitical but essentially political. These differences or similarities between Sorel and Schmitt as stressed by both Kalyvas and Bottici tend to downplay the more antirational and antiliberal dimensions shared by the French and German thinkers. In fact, Sorel also implied that he wanted to believe in his own myths and he did not only present an instrumental view of them. For both Sorel and Schmitt, myth acts as a vehicle for epochal changes, but in Sorel more than in Schmitt, myths have clear apocalyptical implications. Sorel is more convinced of the end of history than Schmitt. But this distinction is mutually affirmed by a shared conviction about the mobilizing force myth and its power to create and affirm enmity. In this context, death and violence in the name of the myth play a central role in the affirmation of the basic antagonisms that for Schmitt define the political.

At the center of this conviction lies the recognition of a historical "parallelism" between Christian martyrs and fighters of the present.[28] Schmitt's view of history is clearly more cyclical, and at times he is more cautious than Sorel about the dangers of mythical violence. But the overpowering nature of political myth led Schmitt to decide that Mussolini represented an avoidable marker of the present and the future. His choice of Mussolini was based not on his belief in a homogenizing ethnic nationalism, as Jürgen Habermas insisted, but on a combination of modern theoretical and historical readings of the past, the present, and the future.[29] To be sure, Schmitt was a convinced anti-Semite before and after 1945. This fact served him well in Nazi times. However, his understanding of history, myth, and antagonism cannot be solely explained by or reduced to his anti-Semitism. As a Catholic member of the revolution against the revolution, Schmitt did not generally conflate in his major works myth and race. Schmitt certainly believed that myths had the power to change and also transcend history, but he did not believe in a single homogenous myth. In her work, Arendt wondered why someone like Schmitt, "whose very ingenious theories about the end of democracy and legal government still make arresting readings," became a "convinced" supporter of National Socialism.[30]

Did Schmitt believe in the Nazis as Arendt suggested or did he strategically decide that they embodied the myth of fascism, that is to say, that they represented a second moment of historical instantiation of the mythical forces that for him were defeating liberalism? In terms of his Sorellian view of things, Schmitt would not have presented both possibilities as mutually exclusive. Ascribing things to myth was not the result of a cold "evaluation" but it was also not the outcome of an entirely unconscious act. It was the result of a decision. For Schmitt, fascist myths acted as what Ernesto Laclau would later think as a "floating signifier," for the people and also for himself. Here, the Sorelian "absolute antithesis" runs parallel to Schmitt's radical understanding of friend-enemy relations in the context of myth. In a world that had relegated liberalism to the past, "authentic adversaries," as represented in the irrational forces of myth, were openly fighting one another. In *The Crisis of Parliamentary Democracy*, myth gave full meaning to politics by establishing a radical form of political animosity. This fundamental enmity was represented in the antithetical choice of Rome or Moscow.[31] Even before the Nazi rise to power, Schmitt had already made his choice.

Before 1933, he preferred the myth of the fascist state to that of a Nazi movement that he strongly opposed and insisted on repressing. Although in his subsequent Nazi writings on state, people, and movement he stressed the role of the latter in the conception of power, that is not what he probably conveyed to Mussolini in his private audience with him in 1936. In fact, Mussolini insisted on the primacy of state over movement and Schmitt seemed to agree. In Mussolini, Schmitt also probably wanted to see a figure of mythical proportions. Of this conversation with the Duce in which "we talked about the relationship between party and state," Schmitt also said: "the conversation with him was a great intellectual pleasure and remains unforgettable in all its details."[32] The opposition between Rome and Moscow and the place of Berlin in it were a key dimension of Schmitt's recollection of his meeting with the dictator.

Mussolini was important to Schmitt, but this importance cannot be exaggerated. He was not his *Katechon*. Schmitt believed in the plural forces of myth, and this belief was a strong element of his attraction to Mussolini. Throughout his life, Schmitt engaged with a plurality of myths that had acquired epochal proportions, that is to say, they had affected the course of history (Hamlet, the Leviathan, the *Katechon*, Mussolini, Hitler and the fascist state, and the nation, among many others, including the careful construction of a myth of himself). These myths explained history but they were also explained through it. They were invented but they also existed. This is one of the meanings behind his long quotation from the Duce in *The Crisis of Parliamentary Democracy*. In 1922 Mussolini had stated: "We have created a myth. This myth is a belief and a passion. It does not need to be a reality. It is a reality in the fact that it is an incitement, that it is a hope, that it is a faith, that it is courage. Our myth is the nation. Our myth is the greatness of the nation. This myth, and this greatness, we want to translate into a complete reality. To them we subordinate everything else."[33] Unlike most fascists, Schmitt did not emulate Mussolini, but he shared with the Duce a converging understanding of the political myth of fascism, a phenomenon both had presented as the emanation of a new energy and a new force. For the Nazi jurist and the fascist dictator, myth was the enactment of a continuum with the transcendental forces of the past as much as the source of the basic form of political antagonism that made politics possible. In 1929, Schmitt approvingly remarked that fascism was "revolutionary" precisely because it overcame the liberal past. The "spirit of fascism" reconnected the present with the classical past, in turn bracketing the Enlightenment and its liberal modernity. In this context, and in contrast with a majority of fascist thinkers, for Schmitt mythos and logos were not dichotomically opposed. As he put it in his early work *Political Romanticism* (1919): "the creation of a political or a historical myth arises from political activity, and the fabric of reasons, which myth cannot forgo either, is the emanation of a political energy."[34]

Schmitt had the conviction that myths constituted historical realities and affirmed new ones. They were the result of conceptualization and, at the same time, they were also real. Schmitt's idea of myth did not pose the return of an old substantial self but the creation of a modern political self articulated in the friend-enemy distinction. Schmitt was not a reactionary but a counter-revolutionary who, at least during the interwar period, saw in fascism an affirmation of the antagonistic politics of the future.

For Schmitt, the myth of the nation and the powerful state that Mussolini represented were part of the new politics he had always advocated for. The reality of the myths of fascism ensured for Schmitt that liberalism would be terminally defeated. Especially in the 1920s and 1930s, his irrationalism depended on the conviction that history was on his side. It is hard to find Schmitt's postwar embracing of the vanquished in his prefascist and fascist works that preceded 1945. In them, his political and historical certainty of the decline of liberalism put him on the side of those he deemed to be its conquerors, first the Italian fascists and then, when it suited him, the Nazis. He had wanted, as he told his Nuremberg interrogators, to provide the German fascists with his own "meaning."[35] If he had been enthusiastic about Italian fascism from the early 1920s, after 1933 he did not find it very hard to convince himself that the Nazis also represented the new winning myth of the century.

But things suddenly changed with the defeat of fascism, and so his conception of myth acquired a deep pessimism. Reflecting on the work of Kafka, Schmitt saw himself as a "child." He had become "the predestinated sacrificial victim of ritual murder, like Kafka's defendant in The Trial. I owe my survival only to the fact that the Lemurs who persecute me are no longer capable of rituals, and therefore no longer ritual killings. That's what saves me."[36]

The notion of a child was important for Schmitt as an image of the defenseless victim of the myths of the conquerors: "All myths of progress are based upon such identifications, that is, upon the childlike assumption that one will be among the gods of the new paradise. In reality, however, the selection process is very rigorous, and the new elites take care to keep a sharper watch than the old. We should thus pause before growing enthusiastic about the new paradise. One cannot yet reasonably say more today."[37]

In his prison writings, Schmitt had criticized his enemies as having false myths that could not recognize the mutual dimension of his own concept of enmity, "in this mutual recognition of acknowledgement lies the greatness of the concept. It is not very appropriate for a mass age with pseudo-theological enemy-myths."[38]

As Andreas Kalyvas and I argued, in his texts from the "cell" Schmitt presented a dual identification. The first was with a literary character, a victim of deception, violence, and impotence who is taken captive and acts against his will, while the second was with a Christianized Greek mythical figure and his tragic, unintended error, which is provoked by manipulation but carried out by desire and love. Both figures, the literary and the mythical, are summoned up in the broader context set by the questions of personal responsibility and moral accountability, which are central to Schmitt. As Kalyvas and I argue, these symbols are complex figures, polysemic and indefinable, and they nonetheless betray a sense a grandeur that is oblivious to other important meanings: oppression, race and gender, and iniquity.[39] Thus in his *Ex Captivitate Salus*, he not only identified with the myth of Benito Cereno and the Christian Epimetheus but also came very close to creating a myth of himself as the embodiment of an old European order that had been defeated.

It is only after the war that he would position himself as the most iconic member of the "defeated." This is the context in which to read his quite underresearched essay on the kernel of historiography: "Historiographia in nuce." In this essay, Schmitt identified with the French thinker Alexis de Tocqueville as a historian of the defeated who had himself been defeated. In praising him for anticipating the change in historical paradigms that awaited the world of the future, Schmitt also suggested that Tocqueville lacked a *Katechon*. In my reading he meant not that the French writer was not reactionary enough but that his masterful reading of history lacked the historical revelatory powers that myths can provide. He had previously charged Juan Donoso Cortés, whom he admired, with the same lack of mythical awareness.[40]

Schmitt criticized nineteenth-century authors for not having his strong eschatological views of the role of myth in history. But does this mean that his ascription to myth led him to stress a view firmly placed out of historical time? Schmitt did not believe that myths were mere illustrations of a personal religion; they were essentially historical tools to read and make changes to the political. This view was more typical of the early twentieth century. First in Georges Sorel and then in Schmitt, this was a view that explicitly normalized apocalyptic thought.

Schmitt's view of the role of myth in history is profoundly immanent. In his most important works, the notion of the enemy in history was more centered on humans than transcendental. This did not change much after 1945. For example, in his dialogues on power and space—two fictional dialogues that Schmitt conceived as a general, more accessible entry to his postwar approach to politics—he presented an antitranscendental view that somewhat ironically brought him back to the position that he had criticized in Tocqueville. As I have argued with Andreas Kalyvas, in the context of the dialogues Schmitt thinks political modernity as being defined by the humanization of power, which coincides with the collapse of ultimate grounds and a widespread recognition of the immanent sources of authority. This historicity of power is central in Schmitt. For him power is rooted in historical human subjectivity and is intrinsic to human relations.[41] I would argue that this does not present a contradiction with his theory of myth since he sees myth as the revealing trait of human subjectivity. Myth makes history human and, at the same time, links the past with vital elements that transcend historical time.

In thinking Schmitt's contested transformation of mythical notions back into history, we should first have in mind that, as Koselleck duly noted, from the time of Herodotus onward, history has been defined by the challenge to historicize myths and legends "as far as it is rationally possible."[42] Schmitt was clearly aware of the historicity of myth, but he went one step further, considering myths not only as metaphors for the location of paradigmatic changes in history but also as living examples of a political time that emanated from the past but also represented the future. Myths were "fragments" of long-standing historical realities that deeply connected humans with their historical existence.[43]

This was one of Schmitt's most Sorellian, and also most fascist, dimensions. These influences he transformed into his own theory of political myth. This theory was original but not exceptional in the sense that it was first formulated in a context of European ideological civil war that, as Enzo Traverso argues, was very different from our own.[44] In this context, key fascist and antifascist thinkers were focused on conceptualizing fascism vis-à-vis political myth.

The question of the centrality of myth in Carl Schmitt is not only fundamental for understanding the thought and context of this key authoritarian, and at times fascist, intellectual. It is also important to inquire more critically into the peculiar place Schmitt occupies in the history and theory of modern political myth.

To be sure, the history of myth has occupied a central role in historiography, notably in historians of Ancient Greece like Jean-Pierre Vernant and Paul Veyne, but in relation to contemporary history, historiographical approaches to political myth tend to adopt a symptomatic path, in turn limiting themselves to the working and functions of the mythical rather than focusing much on myth's relation to modern conceptions of politics. This represents a historiographical oversight, especially for the period of the historiography of the interwar years. This period gave rise to fascism and also to the first theories of modern political myth. It was then that the history of the mythical became a concern, first, for thinkers who endorsed or opposed fascism and, much later, for its historians. In this sense, Schmitt's work represents a key source of its times. First, Schmitt was a powerful agent in the context that motivated modern political myth to emerge as one of the defining terms of fascism, and second, he put forward an interpretation of myth and history that reformulated political theories of modern representative democracy and still remains one of its most influential contestations.

Conclusion

AS ERNST CASSIRER NOTED, political myths were invulnerable insofar as they were impervious to rational arguments. But even if they were absurd or incongruous, they had to be taken seriously. This was not mere intellectual exercise. Cassirer concluded that, rather than being discussed, political mythmaking needed to be understood in order to confront fascism: "In order to fight an *enemy you must know him*." Understanding the myths of fascism implied seeing "the adversary face to face."[1]

Fascists saw in the act of myth-making the ultimate search for an absolute truth. This search involved connecting old myths with new political myths. As Freud had implied and Hitler had stated, fascists also saw in the myth of Prometheus, as well as other classical myths, a clear connection with a golden past. The myth provided a pathway to imagine the present.

In Latin America, one of the most important fascist intellectuals, Leopoldo Lugones, argued that the myth of Prometheus was the key starting point for reading modern Argentine political myths of the nation. The clerico-fascist priest Leonardo Castellani had, in fact, argued that Lugones was "a creator of myths."[2]

Lugones had canonized the most important myth of the nation: the myth of the Gaucho. He later attempted to solidify the myth of Argentina's first modern dictator, General Jose Felix Uriburu. At the same time that he created them, Lugones regarded these myths as entirely true and as the continuation of transhistorical mythical traditions.[3]

In his analysis of Einstein's theory of relativity, Lugones had argued that "the proved does not in itself constitutes a truth." But Lugones was not a relativist but a believer in supreme forms of truth that transcended, and could not be reversed by, corroboration.

Analyzing the centrality of myth in Lugones's Prometheus, Jorge Luis Borges argued that "Lugones rejects the ... tendency to see the foundation of myths in natural phenomena." Thus in his book titled *Lugones*, Borges stated that Lugones "unearths, or rather wants to unearth, the past of truth hidden in myths."[4]

Lugones opposed the need to understand the deep truth of myth to the lack of mythological curiosity in an Argentine society that was "unbalanced" and characterized by "a crisis of immorality, anarchy, and feminism."[5]

The Brazilian fascist leader Plinio Salgado was similarly prompted by mythical thinking, and, like Lugones, he thought that Latin America was destined to be the last vessel for the authoritarian development of the Western tradition. But rather than Prometheus, he wanted to incarnate the myth of Atlantis to expand the Brazilian fascist doctrine of Integralismo into the Latin American continent. He solemnly stated, "we are the last of the West." Salgado saw himself as incarnating the nineteenth-century hero Simon Bolivar. The Brazilian fascist leader stated that "more than ever" the "dream of Bolivar" "shines in the present time." With its "powerful intuition" the myth of Bolivar continued the Atlantis myth. Even though it was not a "total revelation," Bolivarismo showed the way for the future.

Salgado wanted to actualize the myth of Bolivar in his own persona. "Today, meditating on the historical meaning of all that I have done, I feel, in the work I have begun and in which I pursue, the resumption of an abandoned tendency, in this synergistic parallelism in which, more and more, I identify myself, in the most absolute way, to the dream of a man." In short, Salgado wanted to personify the Atlantis myth of Bolivar and his "dream." This integration of the leader's personification of a classic myth with the modern myths of Latin America signaled apocalyptical changes. Latin America was going to prevail over all other parts of the world.[6] Central to the trajectory from the foundation of classic myth to the modern political myth of fascism was the idea that violence as an outcome of the mythical imperative and truth were closely associated.

Irish Blue shirts had chosen the color of their shirts for sacred mythical reasons. It was the color of Ireland's patriot saint. In France, fascists argued that their leader, Henri Doirot, was the personification of Joan of Arc in the mythological past created by the French Parti Populaire.[7] In turn, the Chinese fascists, the blue shirts, argued: "If we cannot use violence to respond to force, then the slogans of liberty, equality, democracy, and liberation can never be realized. China today therefore has no other road to restoration than to use an absolutely revolutionary body as a violent force that supports the principle of nation-first-ism."[8]

Putting the nation first was a way to claim that all others could be put down. Gender, colors, and oceans represented no boundaries to the fascist search for the truth as rooted in the essentially violent forces of the unconscious.

Thus, if the Chinese fascists considered violence the way to achieve the true politics of the people, the fascists of Colombia, the Leopards, asserted, "Violence, as illuminated by the myth of a beautiful and heroic fatherland, is the only thing that can create for us a favorable alternative in the future." Fascists connected violence and death, in and though politics, to a radical renewal of the self rooted in myth.[9]

This overpowering mythical trinity (leader, people, nation) does not require more explanation than the continuous assertion of its existence in the political framework of the fascist project. This myth replaces theory as a practice of individual ascription and collective violence. For the fascists, the repressive and violent hero represents the true theory of myth.

Within this framework, few fascists theorized the myth in the way that liberal antifascists and Marxists did. The exception is the case of the fascist thinker Carl Schmitt. Schmitt stated that "myth is the exegesis of the symbol" but blamed authors like Freud for lacking the symbol. For him, Freud emptied religion in the name of science while performing "rites of de-ghettoization." His critique of the false myths of the enemy was not strategic.

Schmitt's reading of Sorel leads to an analysis of myth as a possibility of an authentic policy, but this policy does not need to be rational or emancipatory, but quite the opposite. The myth serves the purpose of confirming a historicization with theological and sometimes transhistorical overtones. In fact, his text on parliamentarism ends with Mussolini. In this sense, Schmitt seems to propose an idea of incarnation of myth in the sovereign. But he was not unique in doing this. In fascism myths were not metaphorical or symbolic precisely because they were "incarnations."[10]

As the Spanish fascist Ernesto Giménez Caballero stated, fascists had for Mussolini a "mystical and religious reverence." By revering the Duce they learned about their selves.[11] In short, feelings and intuitions were central to the conception of selfhood, the fascist acting-out of the self. The mutual recognition between these two innate aspects of the self necessarily displaced the external and subjective dimensions of reflexivity. As Sergio Panunzio put it, if fascists wanted to "dig deeply" into fascism, they would find that the "soul is the theoretical essence of fascism." For Panunzio thought and action were "the same thing."[12] This conflation of praxis and theory objectified the latter as a mere wording of inner authenticity: "The true man of action . . . is also a theoretician but in a special manner,. . . that is, as an attempt to continually conquer and reconquer the truth through a swift effort of intuition."[13]

In fact, this exercise of searching for the substance of intuitive behavior that is aimed at understanding mythical political incarnation eliminated thinking as a form of theorization in the sense that in fascism concepts were replaced with mythical ideological assumptions. In the traditional meaning of theory, it was not possible "to theorize fascism." As an offspring of war and as action and spirit, fascism represented a "natural regurgitation of currents" (un regurgito naturale di corrente).[14] As uncanny as this equation between vomiting and ideology may sound, its analysis has to be related to the fascist sense of the carnivalistic. In other words, the world upside down that fascism represented in the field of political theory eliminated the need for theory. Libero Merlino, the fascist author of this sentence, explained that fascism had only one theory, "the negation of theory." The theory of fascism was, in fact, the realization in the political sphere of the internal passion that moved fascism to be a "meeting of force." As an externalization of internal currents, fascism turned upside down the field of political theory, or so fascist theorists pretended. Fascism had stolen the subversive dimensions of revolution from socialism without taking its theoretical abstractions. As a new version of older mythical configurations, fascism represented the internal world without the putative artificiality of the external world.

As we saw, Freud considered the myth of Prometheus to be a central dimension of his theory of fascism. For many fascists,

Prometheus represented the dramatic search for the unconscious or as Volt put it, "the tragic impotence of man to find in himself a sense of life."[15] Fascism represented the political answer to this search for meaning. The politicization of this unconscious gave full meaning to the believers.

In short, fascist theory was not connected to external reality, or, to put it differently, it refused to subsume its assumption about the self under the aegis of the reality principle. Indeed, fascists assumed that internal realities were more "real" than the external world.[16] Subjectivity replaced objectivity as a sense of reality.[17] Theory no longer represented a reasoned response to the interaction between subjects, but it was conceived as a rationalization of sentimental acts. This was the fascist sentimental education. Observation impossibly turned inward.

Fascism could never avoid the inescapable fact that it was a critique of ideology and conceptualization from within the world of ideology and conceptualization.

Thus, this radical self-affirmation led to the actual return of basic drives in politics. In this sense, fascism was not only a conceptual form, a way of representing unreason, but also unreason itself, as it unfolded in highly irrational practices. The return of the repressed was not only represented but also actualized in fascist practice.

Freud saw myths having a metaphoric power and he used historical myths as a device to analyze the ideology of fascism. Borges also thought of the myth of fascism as anchored in primordial barbarism. He conceived the peculiar transposition from classical myth to the modern and supposedly secular present as the return of a violent and mythical uncultured past. He adopted an initial ambivalence that led into a deep critical disenchantment. In Borges, as in Freud, the need to detach myth from truth by way of exposing its reliance on liturgy, faith, emotions, and images did not exclude the observations of the trappings of reason. He acutely observed how reason in facing myth not only resorted to argumentation. It was not only that this secular world that Borges envisioned reiterated the classical distinctions between mythos and logos. It also adopted a violent imagination in the figures of mythical leadership. Borges was at the cutting edge of this dual engagement with fascism. Paradoxically, in Borges but also in Freud, the symbolic violence against mythical leaders leads to openness and presumably to democracy.

In Freud the symbolic parricide of the totemic figure of the father lead to the more democratic leadership of the band of brothers. In Borges, the Gods are simply eliminated. For example, in his story "Ragnarök" the Gods make their return in a secular academic world, that of the College of Philosophy and Letters of the University of Buenos Aires (UBA), where Borges was a professor.[18] The return of the Gods first generates joy among the intellectuals that are at that time electing academic authorities, namely, their democratically elected university leaders. But this initial joy recedes once the intellectuals find that the Gods are violent and whimsical beings. We are told that they are also irredeemably deprived of culture; they even look like *malevos* (hoodlums of Buenos Aires), as Borges in a conscious display of his upper-class elitism understands them. Borges himself is among the professors in the story that he also describes as one of his dreams. In the story, after this initial admiration for the Gods, disenchantment with the sacred eventually prevails and leads to radical violence in the name of democracy and secularism. The professors at UBA use their heavy revolvers and "joyfully" kill the Gods. This motif of violence within the myth—a violence that, despite being violently eliminated through the execution of its enablers, remains present as marking a postsecular era of violence for and against myth—is a principal theme in Borges oeuvre. This is especially the case, as we have seen, in his story "Deutsches Requiem," published in the 1940s. For Borges, as for

Freud, myth when it returns to occupy places in the modern secular world is full of suspicions because of its foundational lack of culture, its feral nature, and, above all, its practical denial of reason.

For Borges and Freud the modern transposition of myth is symptomatic of mental structures that were thought to be repressed but that reason cannot accomplish to overcome. For both authors, this symptomatic nature of the myth becomes even more problematic when the mythical explanation became a political cult. The effects of this operation imply violence and death.

While Freud resigns himself to the impossibility of truly eradicating this violence, Borges explores violence as a literary motif. Thus, in contrast with Freud, Borges finds the violence both interesting and attractive as an object of analysis. This is not only a result of his antifascist critique but also part of his interest in a recent mythical past devoid of any political nature. The problem with the *malevos* of his dreams is that they want to become leaders in a secular world rather than the violent figures of the recently gone Buenos Aires of knife fights and duels that he explicitly elevates to mythical nature. But at the same time, Borges treats the hoodlums of his stories as brutal and ignorant figures. He regards them as symbols of the past, relegating their primal violence to an era bypassed by the secular worlds he lives in. These heroes are symbols of the masses. For both Borges and Freud, mythical heroes are tangible or potential expressions of collective unreason. In "Ragnarök," the Gods are "four or five individuals (that) emerged from the mob." This relationship between a mythical authority and the amorphous masses represents the antipopulist dimension of Borges's thought that he will later develop in his not much conceptualized transition from antifascism to anti-Peronism. In the oneiric setting of the story, the faculty election of university authorities highlights the Borgean dichotomy between reason and political myth. After a "centuries-long exile" the Gods are even suspected of not knowing how to talk. They use images and sounds "with something of a gargle and of whistle." The transition from classical to modern political myth appears as "the degeneracy of the Olympic lineage." From being leaders of heroes and men, the Gods become the leaders of the mob. They turned into leaders of poor and inarticulate masses. The Gods were "cunning, ignorant, and cruel like old beasts of prey and. . . . if we let ourselves be overcome by fear or pity, they would finally destroy us."

The killing of the Gods by the faculty of UBA presents learned culture engaging in absolute violence. This preemptive attack is precisely in defense of democratic electoral procedures. It becomes a motif of extreme violence in the name of culture. Borges of course notices the paradox, calling our attention to the fact that the actual killing of the Gods and the instruments of death, the "heavy revolvers," are part of a dream sequence. It is important to note that the rationale behind the violence is not only cultivated but also equally mythical. To put it simply, a mythology of class and race is also present in the Borgean critique of the enemy. The Gods have "very low foreheads, yellow teeth, stringy mulatto or Chinese moustaches, and thick bestial lips." Their clothing "corresponded not to a decorous poverty but rather to the lower luxury [*lujo malevo*] of the gambling houses and brothels of the Bajo."[19]

The Gods of political myth are fueled by ignorance and fear. Their presences foreshadow violence and destruction. They represent foundational violence, but in a modern key they also epitomize the return of an instinctual and mythical barbarism that Borges put into question through an active ironic engagement. It is the written work that conceptualizes what fascist theory refuses to decipher. Borges, like Freud, considered fascism as a mystery insofar as it remains rooted in the mythical. But it is not a mystery that is hard to explain outside of itself. It is only for fascists that fascism cannot be explained in analytic terms. If fascism rejects the written word in order to present itself as mere violent affect, Borges and Freud precisely question this basic premise. Fascism does not represent a program for the future; it is inscribed in the past. For both thinkers, fascism as a living myth can only represent the prehistorical past. This past was the moment when history was not history but myth. For both, fascism has significant transhistorical dimensions. It is the abomination of history and the attempt to return to the world of myth. As we saw, Borges and Freud stress how violence and assassination mark this attempt. In this last regard both Freud and Borges actually perceived and critiqued the self-perception of fascism. Some years before Borges, the Peruvian Marxist Mariátegui had noted that Mussolini felt that he was chosen by "destiny" in order to decree the persecution of the "new God" and reestablish votive offering to the moribund ancient gods.[20]

Fascism was conceived as a disruption of the continuity with change between past and present. However, both authors seemed to share this perception of the mythical dimension of fascism as real and not as a construction. They took the fascist claim to be transhistorical very seriously. To be sure, Borges and Freud signaled the artificial, even pathetic, features of the fascist mythical leadership, especially in the case of Hitler; for both of them fascism was a return of the mythical in the present. It was an actual coming to life of a barbaric political ideology that recuperated primordial violence. Their interpretations that recognized the mythical status of fascism, though obviously not accepting its normative values, voided the historicization of fascism. For most of its historians, fascism invented its mythical subjectivity. But for Borges and Freud, if fascism had elements of stunt and gimmickry, it was not only a conceptual construction but a mythical reality that they openly rejected. They saw fascism at the same time as the political actualization of a fantasy but also a living myth that in its elemental violence, racism, and hierarchies led masses of followers. They moved beyond a functionalist view that cogently highlights the uses of the myth but downplays its ideological dimensions. In this sense, the ironic gaze that both authors adopted to read fascism in its context led them to think the rationale behind the violence of the myth of fascism.[21]

Acknowledgments

THIS BOOK IS DEDICATED to my wife, Laura, and my daughters, Gabriela and Lucia. Like all books, this one has a long list of readers who read many of its parts before the actual book appeared. With their ideas and support they made it possible.

First, I want to thank my students of the New School for Social Research and Lang College also at the New School. Second, I want to thank all the colleagues who motivated me to think about these issues beyond a perspective (important and at the same time limited) that considers the myth as a function of something else.

I would especially like to thank my editor at Columbia University, Wendy Lochner, for her patience and continuing support over the years. I also want to thank Professor Amy Allen.

I also thank Robert Demke for his copyediting and Emmanuel Guerisoli for the preparation of the index.

I also thank my parents, Norma and Jaime, and my siblings, Ines and Diego.

I have presented some of the contents of this book in Germany, Argentina, Mexico, the United States, Spain, Uruguay, Brazil, and Italy. When I was finishing the draft, I was invited to teach a seminar on the history of political myth at Technische Universität Dresden.

At the New School, where I have been teaching history since 2006, I presented my text on Freud in the framework of its venerable General Seminar in a now "mythical" building that no longer exists and at a table and in a chair that are no longer there. I vividly remember that the philosopher Richard Bernstein, who invited me to present at the seminar, said a few words that marked me deeply. Before my presentation he told me (not without irony) two things that gave me encouragement, but that also worried me. First, Dick said that it was there, in that same seminar, that Hannah Arendt had presented her work.

Second, he congratulated me for having chosen a theme (Freud) about which everyone present could give an opinion and also criticize me with authority and severity. Of course, my presentation was criticized in both ways by those present at the distinguished seminar, and I believe that this motivated me to stick to my guns as well as to reformulate some of my theses.

I would like to thank many colleagues and friends who read a part, or parts, of this book, especially Amy Allen, Andrew Arato, Ben Brower, Amy Chazkel, Juan De Castro, Emmanuel Guerisoli, Luis Herrán Ávila, Andreas Kalyvas, Nara Milanich, Pablo Piccato, Caterina Pizzigoni, Matthew Specter, Angelo Ventrone, Enzo Traverso, and Eli Zaretsky.

I would also like to thank my colleagues: Richard Bernstein, Chiara Bottici, Oz Frankel, the late Ágnes Heller, Jeremy Varon, Nancy Fraser, Andreas Kalyvas, James Miller and Ann Laura Stoler, and Eli Zaretsky. I want to thank Alicia Borinsky, Fabian Bosoer, Bruno Bosteels, José Emilio Burucúa, Roger Chartier, the late Tulio Halperín Donghi, Dominick LaCapra, María Pía Lara, Jeffrey Mehlman, José Moya, Elías Palti, Mariano Plotkin, Raanan Rein, Michael P. Steinberg, Héctor Raúl Solis Gadea, Doris Sommer, Alberto Spektorowski, and Nadia Urbinati.

Past dialogues with my dear friend and teacher, the late José Sazbón and his frank and profound criticism are also part of this book. Several earlier versions of different chapters were published in Mariano Plotkin and Joy Damousi, eds., *The Transnational Unconscious* (London: Palgrave Macmillan, 2009); in *Dapim—Studies on the Holocaust* 25 (2011); in my book *El canon del Holocausto* (Buenos Aires: Prometeo, 2010); and in Adriana Brodsky and Raanan Rein, eds., *The New Cultural History of Jewish Argentina* (Leiden: Brill, 2013). My first book on the myth of the Argentine dictator, the general José Félix Uriburu (FCE, 2002), represents the first text of what, I believe, is a long personal journey in which my perspectives as a citizen and my deep interest in Freud and Borges began to overlap. But the study of classical myths and modern political myths is not only part of academic life. I have discussed myth and mythologies with my daughters Lucia and Gabriela. In particular, we have read the beautiful version of Greek myths by the Argentine writer Ana María Shúa. Before, when they were toddlers, we did not discuss these themes, but even at an early age they both recognized the face of Freud on the cover of his texts and made blocks with the books of Borges that have long populated my library and that with the passing of the years also inspired this book.

Notes

Preface

1. Benito Mussolini, "Il discorso di Napoli," in *Opera Omnia* (Florence: La Fenice, 1951–1962), 38:457.
2. See Federico Finchelstein, *A Brief History of Fascist Lies* (Oakland: University of California Press, 2020).
3. On fascism, see Federico Finchelstein, *From Fascism to Populism in History* (Oakland: University of California Press, 2017). See also see Zeev Sternhell, *Ni droite ni gauche: l'idéologie fasciste en France* (Paris: Gallimard, 2012); Robert Paxton, *The Anatomy of Fascism* (New York: Vintage, 2005); Geoff Eley, *Nazism as Fascism: Violence, Ideology and the Ground of Consent in Germany* (London: Routledge, 2013); António Costa Pinto, *The Nature of Fascism Revisited* (Boulder: Social Science Monographs, 2012); Angelo Ventrone, *La seduzione totalitaria: guerra, modernità, violenza politica, 1914–1918* (Roma: Donzelli, 2003); Emilio Gentile, *Fascismo: storia e interpretazione* (Rome: Laterza, 2002). On fascism and violence, see Giulia Albanese, "Brutalization and Violence to the Origins of Fascism," *Studi storici* 1 (2014): 3–14; Ruth Ben-Ghiat, *Strongmen: Mussolini to the Present* (New York: Norton, 2020). On fascism and myth, see especially the works of George Mosse and Jason Stanley. See George Mosse, *The Fascist Revolution: Toward a General Theory of Fascism* (New York: Howard Fertig, 1999); and Jason Stanley, *How Fascism Works: The Politics of Us and Them* (New York: Random House, 2018).
4. I have studied these dimensions in Finchelstein, *A Brief History of Fascist Lies*.

5. Hannah Arendt, *The Burden of Our Time* (London: Martin Secker and Warburg, 1951), 434–435.

1. Myth and Fascism

1. Jorge Luis Borges, "Mitologías del odio," *Critica*, September 29, 1933; Jorge Luis Borges, *Textos Recobrados 1931–1955* (Buenos Aires: Sudamericana, 2011), 51–52.

2. Theodor Adorno, *Minima Moralia* (New York: Verso, 2005), 71.

3. Adorno, 71, 72.

4. Hannah Arendt, "Ideology and Terror: A Novel Form of Government," *Review of Politics* 15, no. 3 (1953): 303–327.

5. Ernst Cassirer, *The Myth of the State* (New York: Doubleday, 1955 [1946]), 55, 363, 365.

6. Hugo Francisco Bauza, *Que es un mito: una aproximación a la mitología clásica* (Buenos Aires: FCE, 2012), 19. Gershom Scholem also stresses the antinormative dimensions of myth as well as its antimetaphorical tendencies. The mythical world finds its expression in images and symbols. He notes its central anthropomorphic elements and its pantheistic unification of the realms of God, Cosmos, and man. In short, Scholem opposed the symbolic nature of myth to rationalistic thinking and abstraction. See Gershom Scholem, "*Kabbalah* and *Myth*," in *On the Kabbalah and Its Symbolism* (New York: Schocken, 1977), 88. See also Moshe Idel, "Function of Symbols in Gershom Scholem," in *Old Words, New Mirrors, on Jewish Mysticism* (Philadelphia: University of Pennsylvania Press, 2010), 36.

7. Jean-Pierre Vernant, *Myth and Thought Among the Greeks* (New York: Zone, 2006), 136, 119.

8. Jean-Pierre Vernant, *Entre mito y política* (Mexico: Fondo de Cultura Económica, 2002), 10. See also, on myth in modern history, Hans Blumenberg, *Work on Myth* (Cambridge, MA: MIT Press, 1985); Chiara Bottici, *A Philosophy of Political Myth* (Cambridge: Cambridge University Press, 2007); José Emilio Burucúa, *El mito de Ulises en el mundo moderno* (Buenos Aires: Eudeba, 2013); María Pía Lara, *The Disclosure of Politics: Struggles Over the Semantics of Secularization* (New York: Columbia University Press, 2013).

9. Inga Clendinnen, *Ambivalent Conquests* (New York: Cambridge University Press, 1987); Paul Veyne, *Did the Greeks Believe in Their Myths?* (Chicago: University of Chicago Press, 1988); Irene Silverblatt, *Moon,*

Sun and Witches: Gender, Ideology and Class in Inca and Colonial Peru (Princeton: Princeton University Press, 1987).

10. Zeev Sternhell, *The Anti-Enlightenment Tradition* (New Haven, CT: Yale University Press, 2010). On the centrality of Sternhell's work, see Finchelstein, "Trump's Mount Rushmore Speech Is the Closest He's Come to Fascism," *Foreign Policy*, July 8, 2020.

11. See Juan Donoso Cortés, *Obras de Don Juan Donoso Cortés* (Madrid: Sociedad Editorial de San Francisco de Sales, 1901), 1:281.

12. See Juan Donoso Cortés, "Carta al Director del Heraldo, Paris 15 de Abril de 1852," in *Obras de Don Juan Donoso Cortés*, 2:312–315.

13. See Cortés, *Obras de Don Juan Donoso Cortés*, 1:205–209.

14. See Thomas Carlyle, *Latter-Day Pamphlets* (1850), in *Collected Works* (London, 1870), 19:113–115, 134–136. See also Carlyle, *On Heroes, Hero-Worship, and the Heroic in History: Six Lectures* (London: James Fraser, 1841). On Carlyle's theory of history and its relation to charisma, see David A. Bell, *Men on Horseback: The Power of Charisma in the Age of Revolution* (New York: Farrar, Straus and Giroux, 2020), 219–220.

15. On the idea of virtuosity in classical myth, see Pierre Vidal-Naquet, *Fragments sur l'art antique* (Paris: Agnès Viénot Éditions, 2002), 59–61. On the militarization of myth and its connection to Nazism, see Carlo Ginzburg, *Clues, Myths, and the Historical Method* (Baltimore: Johns Hopkins University Press, 2013), 114–131.

16. Benito Mussolini, "Il discorso di Napoli," in *Opera Omnia* (Florence: La Fenice, 1951–1962), 38:457.

17. Carl Schmitt, *The Crisis of Parliamentary Democracy* (Cambridge, MA: MIT Press, 1985), 76. See also Simonetta Falasca-Zamponi, *Fascist Spectacle: The Aesthetics of Power in Mussolini's Italy* (Berkeley: University of California Press, 1997), 219; Georges Sorel, *Reflections on Violence* (New York: Peter Smith, 1941). Georg Lukacs also stressed this connection between Sorel and the "myth of fascism." See his polemic book, *The Destruction of Reason* (New York: Verso 2021), 32, and the preface by Enzo Traverso.

18. See Piero Gobetti, "Benito Mussolini," in *On Liberal Revolution* (New Haven, CT: Yale University Press, 2000), 58. On fascism and history, see Claudio Fogu, *The Historic Imaginary: Politics of History in Fascist Italy* (Toronto: University of Toronto Press, 2003).

19. See Borges, *Obras Completas* (Barcelona: Emecé, 1996), 4:37–41.

20. See Georges Bataille, *Visions of Excess* (Minneapolis: University of Minnesota Press, 1985), 137–160. On Bataille, see Carolyn J. Dean, *The Self and Its Pleasures: Bataille, Lacan, and the History of the Decentered Subject* (Ithaca: Cornell University Press, 1992).

21. Sigmund Freud, "Some Elementary Lessons in Psycho-Analysis," in *Collected Papers* (London: Hogarth, 1957), 5:382.

22. For analysis of the notion of the return of the repressed in relation to fascist ideology and practice, see Dominick LaCapra, *Representing the Holocaust: History, Theory, Trauma* (Ithaca, NY: Cornell University Press, 1994).

23. See Max Horkheimer and Theodor W. Adorno, *Dialectic of Enlightenment* (Stanford: Stanford University Press, 2002), xvi.

24. See Horkheimer and Adorno, 164.

25. See Sigmund Freud, "Why War?" (1932), in *Collected Papers*, 5:283.

26. Letter to Ernest Jones, March 2, 1937, in *The Complete Correspondence of Sigmund Freud and Ernest Jones, 1908–1939*, ed. R. Andrew Paskauskas (Cambridge: Belknap Press of Harvard University Press, 1993), 757.

27. Axel Honneth, *Pathologies of Reason: On the Legacy of Critical Theory* (New York: Columbia University Press, 2009), 127–128.

28. Letter to Romain Rolland, March 4, 1923, in *The Letters of Sigmund Freud*, ed. Ernst L. Freud (New York: Basic, 1960), 341–342.

29. Eli Zaretsky, *Secrets of the Soul: A Social and Cultural History of Psychoanalysis* (New York: Knopf, 2004), 229, 245, 229.

30. For some illuminating examples, see Eli Zaretsky, *Political Freud: A History* (New York: Columbia University Press, 2017); Dominick LaCapra, *History and Its Limits: Human, Animal, Violence* (Ithaca: Cornell University Press, 2009); María Pía Lara, *Narrating Evil: A Postmetaphysical Theory of Reflective Judgment* (New York: Columbia University Press, 2007); Richard J. Bernstein, *Radical Evil: A Philosophical Interrogation* (Cambridge: Polity, 2002); Bruno Bosteels, *Marx and Freud in Latin America: Politics, Religion, and Psychoanalysis in the Age of Terror* (New York: Verso, 2012); Michael Steinberg, *Judaism Musical and Unmusical* (Chicago: University of Chicago Press, 2008); Mariano Plotkin and Joy Damousi, eds., *The Transnational Unconscious* (London: Palgrave Macmillan, 2009); Amy Allen, *Critique on the Couch: Why Critical Theory Needs Psychoanalysis* (New York: Columbia University Press, 2020); Daniel Pick, *The Pursuit of the Nazi Mind* (Oxford: Oxford University Press, 2012). For some key studies of myth vis-à-vis the histories of fascism and anti-Semitism, see Ian Kershaw, *The "Hitler Myth": Image and Reality in the Third Reich* (Oxford: Oxford University Press, 1987); Antonio Cazorla, *Franco, biografía del mito* (Madrid: Alianza, 2015); Joan Maria Thomàs, *José Antonio Primo de Rivera: The Reality and Myth of a Spanish Fascist Leader* (New York: Berghahn, 2019); Emilio Gentile, *Il mito dello stato nuovo dall'antigiolittismo al fascismo* (Rome: Laterza, 1982); Paul Hanebrink, *A Spectre Haunting Europe: The Myth of Judeo-Bolshevism* (Cambridge, MA:

Harvard University Press, 2018); Mark Antliff, *Avant-Garde Fascism: The Mobilization of Myth, Art, and Culture in France, 1909–1939* (Durham, NC: Duke University Press, 2007).

31. "En el principio de la literatura está el mito, y asimismo en el fin." Borges, "Parábola de Cervantes y de Quijote," in *Obras Completas*, 2:177.

32. "Es el crematorio -dijo alguien-. Adentro está la cámara letal. Dicen que la inventó un filántropo cuyo nombre, creo, era Adolfo Hitler." Borges, "Utopía de un hombre que está cansado," in *Obras Completas*, 3:56.

33. Blumenberg, *Work on Myth*, 34–58; Cassirer, *The Myth of the State*, 54–55.

34. Arendt, "Ideology and Terror"; Arendt, *The Origins of Totalitarianism* (New York: Meridian, 1959), 158–184; Arendt, "The Seeds of a Fascist International," in *Essays in Understanding, 1930–1954*, ed. Jerome Kohn (New York: Harcourt Brace, 1994), 147.

35. Borges, "Anotación al 23 de Agosto de 1944," in *Obras Completas*, 2:105. When an English translation of Borges is not cited, the translations from the Spanish are my own.

36. Lara, *Narrating Evil*.

37. I am making reference to a suggestive argument by Ann Laura Stoler, "Carceral Archipelagos of Empire: Retracing the Imperial Modern," presented at the conference "On Camps: History, Violence and Trauma," at the History Department of the New School for Social Research and Eugene Lang College, New York, October 14, 2010. For a genealogical analysis of the Holocaust and colonialism, see Enzo Traverso, *The Origins of Nazi Violence* (New York: New Press, 2003). See also A. Dirk Moses, *The Problems of Genocide: Permanent Security and the Language of Transgression* (Cambridge University Press, 2021); Dan Stone, *Histories of the Holocaust* (Oxford: Oxford University Press, 2010), chap. 5. On the violence of imperial formation, see Benjamin Brower, *A Desert Named Peace: The Violence of France's Empire in the Algerian Sahara, 1844–1902* (New York: Columbia University Press, 2009).

38. See Étienne Balibar, *We, the People of Europe?: Reflections on Transnational Citizenship* (Princeton: Princeton University Press, 2004), 2.

39. Steinberg, *Judaism Musical and Unmusical*, 55–56.

40. Jürgen Habermas, *The Philosophical Discourse of Modernity* (Cambridge, MA: MIT Press, 1987), 216.

41. Piero Meldini, *Mussolini contro Freud: la psicoanalisi nella pubblicistica fascista* (Firenze: Guaraldi, 1976); and Federico Finchelstein, *A Brief History of Fascist Lies* (Oakland: University of California Press, 2020).

42. Virgilio Filippo, *Los judíos: Juicio histórico científico que el autor no pudo transmitir por L.R.S. Radio Paris* (Buenos Aires: Tor, 1939), 219.

43. Alberto Spaini, "Abasso Freud," *L'Idea nazionale*, November 21, 1925, 3; Finchelstein, *A Brief History of Fascist Lies.*

44. See Benito Mussolini, "Labirinto comunista," in *Opera Omnia*, 26:11–12; Finchelstein, *A Brief History of Fascist Lies.*

45. See Jorge Luis Borges, *Leopoldo Lugones*, in *Obras Completas en Colaboración* (Barcelona: Emecé, 1997), 489, 492–493; Leopoldo Lugones, *Prometeo (Un proscripto del sol)* (Buenos Aires: Otero, 1910), 5, 241, 260, 283–284; Leopoldo Lugones, *El Payador* (Buenos Aires: Otero Impresores, 1916), 6.

46. See Leopoldo Lugones, "La formación del ciudadano," *La Nación*, February 13, 1938. See also Federico Finchelstein, *Transatlantic Fascism: Ideology, Violence, and the Sacred in Argentina and Italy, 1919–1945* (Durham, NC: Duke University Press, 2010), 286–287, 317, 154–155, 175.

47. Finchelstein, *A Brief History of Fascist Lies*, 21, 37, 58–74.

48. For an analysis of the many paradoxes facing this contextual subject position, see Agnes Heller, *A Theory of Modernity* (Oxford: Blackwell, 1999) 140.

49. See Jürgen Habermas, *The Divided West* (Cambridge, MA: Polity, 2006), chap. 4.

50. Peter Gay, *Freud: A Life for Our Time* (New York: Norton, 1988) 628; Ernest Jones, *The Life and Work of Sigmund Freud* (New York: Basic, 1957), 3:226.

2. Freud, Fascism, and the Return of the Myth

1. For Ernest Jones's description of the meeting, see Ernest Jones, *The Life and Work of Sigmund Freud* (New York: Basic, 1957), 3:180. Edoardo Weiss had a slightly different version of the events. See Edoardo Weiss, *Sigmund Freud as a Consultant* (New Brunswick, NJ: Transaction, 1991), 20–21. Freud presented Weiss as "my friend and pupil." See Freud, *The Standard Edition of the Complete Psychological Works of Sigmund Freud*, ed. James Strachey (London: Hogarth, 1961), 21:256.

2. This, of course, was not enough and the *Italian Journal of Psychoanalysis* was banned by the end of 1933, a year of great anti-Semitic agitation in fascist Italy. One year later Freud thought about the Forzano-Weiss connection regarding the ban. He wrote: "Although Weiss has direct access to Mussolini and received from him a favorable promise, the ban could not be lifted." Letter To Arnold Zweig, September 30, 1934, in *The Letters of Sigmund Freud*, ed. Ernst L. Freud (New York: Basic, 1960), 421–422. On the history of Italian psychoanalysis, see Michel David, *La psicoanalisi*

nella cultura italiana (Turin: Boringhieri, 1970). On the history of Italian fascist anti-Semitism, see Enzo Collotti, *Il fascismo e gli ebrei: le leggi razziali in Italia* (Rome: Laterza, 2003); Michele Sarfatti, *Gli ebrei nell'Italia fascista: vicende, identità, persecuzione* (Turin: Einaudi, 2000); Renzo De Felice, *Storia degli ebrei italiani sotto il fascismo* (Turin: Einaudi, 1993); Meir Michaelis, *Mussolini and the Jews: German, Italian Relations and the Jewish Question in Italy, 1922–1945* (Oxford: Clarendon, 1978); Marie-Anne Matard-Bonucci, *L'Italie fasciste et la persécution des juifs* (Paris: Perrin, 2007); Valeria Galimi, *Sottogliocchi di tutti: la società italiana elepersecuzioni controgli ebrei* (Florence: Le Monnier, 2018); Simon Levis Sullam, *I carnefici italiani: scene dal genocidio degli ebrei, 1943–1945* (Milan: Feltrinelli, 2015). On fascist racism, see also the study by Aaron Gillette, *Racial Theories in Fascist Italy* (London: Routledge, 2002).

3. He would later tell Ernst Jones: "Unfortunately the power that has hitherto protected us—Mussolini—now seems to be giving Germany a free hand." Letter to Ernest Jones, March 2, 1937, in *The Complete Correspondence of Sigmund Freud and Ernest Jones, 1908–1939*, ed. R. Andrew Paskauskas (Cambridge: Belknap Press of Harvard University Press, 1993), 757.

4. Michael Molnar, ed., *The Diary of Sigmund Freud, 1929–1939* (New York: Maxwell Macmillan, 1992), 141.

5. "Benito Mussolini mit dem ergebenen Gruss eines alten Mannes der im Machthaber den Kultur Heros erkennt." See the quotation in Weiss, *Sigmund Freud as a Consultant*, 20. See also Jones, *The Life and Work of Sigmund Freud*, 3:180.

6. Letter to George Sylvester Viereck, July 20, 1928, in Freud, *The Letters of Sigmund Freud*, 234. In 1923, however, when he visited Rome, Freud did not mention fascism at all. See letter to Ernest Jones, September 23, 1923, in Paskauskas, *The Complete Correspondence of Sigmund Freud and Ernest Jones*, 527.

7. Carl E. Schorske, *Fin-de-siècle Vienna: Politics and Culture* (New York: Knopf, 1980).

8. I want to thank Eli Zaretsky for sharing with me his criticism of the image of the "liberal" Freud. The best and most intelligent example of this "liberal" approach is Peter Gay, *Freud: A Life for Our Time* (New York: Norton, 1988). For an analysis of the historiography of psychoanalysis, see Michael Steinberg, *Judaism Musical and Unmusical* (Chicago: University of Chicago Press, 2008).

9. Ironically, as Michael Steinberg notes, nothing was more Viennese than Freud's disdain for Vienna. See Steinberg, *Judaism Musical and Unmusical*. On how the Austrian context shaped Freud's global understanding,

see Steinberg, "The Catholic Culture of the Austrian Jews," in *Austria as Theater and Ideology: The Meaning of the Salzburg Festival* (Ithaca, NY: Cornell University Press, 2000).

10. In his subtle analysis of Freud's Moses, the late Edward Said, like his colleague Yosef Yerushalmi before him, seems to be nonetheless engaged in these binaries. As Michael Steinberg argues with respect to Said, he is "less willing to disavow the very idea of identity, the very idea of a boundary." See Steinberg, *Judaism Musical and Unmusical*. See also Yosef Hayim Yerushalmi, *Freud's Moses: Judaism Terminable and Interminable* (New Haven, CT: Yale University Press, 1991); and Edward Said, *Freud and the Non-European* (London: Verso, 2003).

11. Dominick LaCapra, *Writing History, Writing Trauma* (Baltimore: Johns Hopkins University Press, 2000).

12. Letter to Ernest Jones, August 23, 1933, in Paskauskas, *The Complete Correspondence of Sigmund Freud and Ernest Jones*, 726. Some years later he wrote to Stefan Zweig in 1937: "The immediate future looks grim, for psychoanalysis as well. In any case I am not likely to experience anything enjoyable during the weeks and months I may still have to live." Letter to Stefan Zweig, October 17, 1937, in Freud, *The Letters of Sigmund Freud*, 438.

13. Enzo Traverso, *Fire and Blood: The European Civil War* (New York: Verso, 2016).

14. On the subject position of exile, see Enzo Traverso, *La pensée dispersée: figures de l'exil judéo-allemand* (Paris: Léo Scheer, 2004). See also the classic section by Hannah Arendt, "Between Pariah and Parvenu," in *The Origins of Totalitarianism* (New York: Meridian, 1959), 56–68.

15. Steinberg, *Judaism Musical and Unmusical*, 55–56. As Richard Bernstein has argued, Freud provided key insights regarding the Nazi interest in reviving polytheistic mythology. See Richard Bernstein, *Freud and the Legacy of Moses* (Cambridge: Cambridge University Press, 1998), 76.

16. On this topic see Eli Zaretsky, *Secrets of the Soul: A Social and Cultural History of Psychoanalysis* (New York: Knopf, 2004), 244–245. For an analysis of the position of the "established" and the "outsider" in modern society, see Norbert Elias, "Notes sur les juifs en tant que participant á une relation établis-marginaux," in *Norbert Elias par lui-même* (Paris: Agora, 1991). See also Norbert Elias, *The Civilizing Process: Sociogenetic and Psychogenetic Investigations* (Oxford: Blackwell, 2000). For an analysis of Elias in this context, see Roger Chartier, "Elias, proceso de la civilización y barbarie," in *El Holocausto, los alemanes y la culpa colectiva: el debate Goldhagen*, ed. Federico Finchelstein (Buenos Aires: Eudeba/Buenos Aires University Press, 1999). This antifascist dimension of

Freud has also been present in the work of Michel Foucault. As Élisa-beth Roudinesco cogently reminds us. "In its essence, he [Foucault] argued, psychoanalysis [is] in theoretical and political opposition to fascism—even if its practitioners are not. In providing sexuality with a law, and demarcating itself from the racism of theories of inequality, it has also had the merit of distrusting all procedures for controlling and managing everyday sexuality. In short, Foucault attributed a 'political honour' to psychoanalysis as a discipline, and to Freud's invention a capacity for exposing the mechanisms of the dominant power by means of doubt." Élisabeth Roudinesco, *Lacan: In Spite of Everything* (London: Verso, 2014). See note 32.

17. Sigmund Freud, *Moses and Monotheism* (New York: Vintage, 1939), 144–145.
18. Here, I appropriate Jacques Lacan's notion of Nazism as a "resurgence" of sacrifice and "a monstrous spell." See Jacques Lacan, *The Four Fundamental Concepts of Psycho-Analysis* (New York: Norton, 1981), 275.
19. Slavoj Žižek, *Did Somebody Say Totalitarianism?: Five Interventions in the (Mis)use of a Notion* (New York: Verso, 2001), 44.
20. For Hannah Arendt's understanding of ideological thinking as the inca-pacity to think, see Arendt, "Ideology and Terror: A Novel Form of Government," *Review of Politics* 15, no. 3 (1953): 303–327; Arendt, *The Origins of Totalitarianism*, 158–184.
21. See my critique of Arendt, in Federico Finchelstein, *A Brief History of Fascist Lies* (Oakland: University of California Press, 2020), 18, 89.
22. See Zaretsky, *Secrets of the Soul*, 245. See also Hannah Arendt, "The Seeds of a Fascist International," in *Essays in Understanding, 1930–1954*, ed. Jerome Kohn (New York: Harcourt Brace, 1994), 146–147.
23. "My correspondence with Einstein has been published simultaneously in German, French, and English, but it can be neither advertised nor sold in Germany." Letter to Oskar Pfister, May 28, 1933, in Freud, *The Letters of Sigmund Freud*, 417.
24. See Sigmund Freud, "Why War?" (1932), in *Collected Papers* (London: Hogarth, 1957), 5:273–287. For a previous Freudian elaboration of this topic, see Sigmund Freud, *Reflections on War and Death* (New York: Moffat, Yard, 1918), 37.
25. See Zeev Sternhell, with Mario Sznajder and Maia Asheri, *The Birth of Fascist Ideology: From Cultural Rebellion to Political Revolution* (Princeton: Princeton University Press, 1994), 254; Piero Melograni, "The Cult of the Duce in Mussolini's Italy," *Journal of Contemporary History* 11, no. 4 (1976): 221–237. As Falasca Zamponi argues, Freud wrote the dedication in a very

specific situation. See Simonetta Falasca-Zamponi, *Fascist Spectacle: The Aesthetics of Power in Mussolini's Italy* (Berkeley: University of California Press, 1997), 53; Weiss explained the dedication as a result of Freud's putative admiration for the Roman archeological excavations Mussolini had ordered at the time. Giovacchino Forzano and Peter Gay seemed to believe that Mussolini, having in mind the dedication, had intervened with Hitler on Freud's behalf, a fact strongly denied by Weiss in his *Sigmund Freud as a Consultant*, 20, 22–21. For his part, the Italian historian Renzo de Felice cites a letter where Forzano asked Mussolini in 1938 to intercede for Freud with Hitler. De Felice suggests that Mussolini did this but without success. See Renzo De Felice, *Mussolini il duce: gli anni del consenso, 1929–1936* (Turin: Einaudi, 1996) 34. On Italian psychoanalysis under fascism, see David, *La psicoanalisi nella cultura italiana*; Mauro Pasqualini, "Origin, Rise, and Destruction of a Psychoanalytic Culture in Fascist Italy, 1922–1938," in *Psychoanalysis and Politics*, ed. Joy Damousi and Mariano Plotkin (New York: Oxford University Press, 2012); Roberto Zapperi, *Freud e Mussolini: la psicoanalisi in Italia durante il regime fascista* (Milan: Franco Angeli, 2013); Maddalena Carli, "Saluti da Vienna, o duce," *Il Manifesto*, September 25, 2014.

26. I have analyzed the relations between fascism and psychoanalysis in my book *A Brief History of Fascist Lies*; Finchelstein, *The Ideological Origins of the Dirty War: Fascism, Populism, and Dictatorship in Twentieth Century Argentina* (Oxford: Oxford University Press, 2014), 43, 56, 102, 115, 119, 145–147.

27. See Saul Friedlander, *Nazi Germany and the Jews: The Years of Persecution, 1933–1939* (New York: Harper Perennial, 1998), 57.

28. Molnar, *The Diary of Sigmund Freud*, 149.

29. Raul Hilberg, *The Destruction of the European Jews* (New York: Holmes and Meier, 1985), 5–28. For an analysis of Hilberg, see Federico Finchelstein, "The Holocaust Canon: Rereading Raul Hilberg," *New German Critique* 96 (2005–2006).

30. Freud, *Moses and Monotheism*, 117. On Nazism and Christianity, see Susannah Heschel, *The Aryan Jesus: Christian Theologians and the Bible in Nazi Germany* (Princeton: Princeton University Press, 2008); Richard Steigmann-Gall, *The Holy Reich: Nazi Conceptions of Christianity, 1919–1945* (Cambridge: Cambridge University Press, 2003).

31. Letter to Max Eitingon, January 17, 1938, Freud, *The Letters of Sigmund Freud*, 440.

32. Benito Mussolini, "La dottrina del fascismo," in *Opera Omnia* (Florence: La Fenice, 1951–1962), 34:119–121.

33. Jones, *The Life and Work of Sigmund Freud*, 3:184.

34. See Agnes Heller, *A Theory of Modernity* (Oxford: Blackwell, 1999), 197–199.

35. On the notion of founding trauma, see LaCapra, *Writing History, Writing Trauma*, 81.

36. Giuseppe Bottai, "Disciplina," *Critica Fascista* (July 15, 1923): 45–47.

37. Nino Sammartano, "Contro la possibilità di un esperimento democratico del fascismo," *Critica Fascista* (December 15, 1925): 463. See also Benito Mussolini, "Maschere e volto della Germania," *Gerarchia* (March 1922): 3.

38. See *Gerarchia* (October 1941): 557. Many texts were dedicated to the exegesis of Mussolini's work as action: see, for example, Hermann Ellwanger, *Sulla lingua di Mussolini* (Verona: Mondadori, 1941).

39. Oddone Fattini, "Revoluzionari nello spirito e nell' azione," *Universalità fascista* (February 1934): 205.

40. See Enrico Corradini, "L'agape sacra," *Il Popolo d'Italia*, March 22, 1924.

41. Roberto Mazzetti, "Proletariato e lotta di clase," *Meridiani* (April-May 1936): 14. See also Alberto Di Stefani, "Vilfredo Pareto," *Gerarchia* (August 1923): 1189.

42. La Direzione, "Proponimento," *Critica Fascista* (July 15, 1923): 45–47.

43. "Non si può compiere nulla di grande se non si è in istato di amorosa passione, in istato di misticismo religioso." Mussolini, *Opera omnia*, 19:439.

44. Mario Rivoire, "Mistica fascista e mistica totalitaria," *Gerarchia* (March 1940): 128–132.

45. Gaetano Salvemini, *The Origins of Fascism in Italy* (New York: Harper and Row, 1973), 301. On Salvemini, see Renato Camurri, "Introduzione," in *Lettere Americane 1927–1949*, by Gaetano Salvemini, ed. Renato Camurri (Rome: Donzelli, 2015).

46. Fernando Mezzasoma, "Volontarismo Golliardico," *Meridiani* (January 1936): 7.

47. L'imperialismo è il fondamento della vita per ogni popolo che tende a espandersi economicamente e spiritualmente," discorso di piazza San Sepolcro del 23 marzo 1919, in Mussolini, *Opera omnia*, 12:323.

48. "L'imperialismo è la legge eterna e immutabile della vita. Esso in fondo non è che il bisogno, il desiderio e la volontà di espansione che ogni individuo, che ogni popolo vivo e vitale ha in sé." Mussolini, *Opera omnia*, 12:101.

49. See Enrico Corradini, "Il residuo e la vita," *Il Popolo d'Italia*, November 8, 1923; Corradini, "Il parassita," *Il Popolo d'Italia*, December 27, 1923; Corradini, "I nostri maestri," *Il Popolo d'Italia*, May 17, 1923; Corradini, "Le

due nature del liberalismo," *Il Popolo d'Italia*, October 21, 1923; Corradini, "Solennità della Patria," *Il Popolo d'Italia*, October 27, 1923.

50. See Arrigo Solmi, "Il fascismo e lo sviluppo della coscienza nazionale," *Gerarchia* (January 1923): 673.

51. See "Le fonti della rivoluzione," *Il Popolo d'Italia*, January 20, 1928. As Armando Carlini had earlier put it in 1920, true freedom was the result of searching for the profound laws of the self. Carlini, "Il Pensiero e la vita," in *Giornale critico della filosofia italiana*, ed. Giovanni Gentile (Messina: Giuseppe Principato, 1920), 1:380–382.

52. Camillo Pellizzi, "Le maschere e il volto della rivoluzione," *Il Popolo d'Italia*, May 10, 1923. See also Enrico Corradini, "Sato debole, nazione serva," *Il Popolo d'Italia*, March 1, 1925.

53. Antonio Renda, "La dittatura per la *libertà*," *Critica Fascista* (November 1, 1923): 191–192.

54. "L'elevato discorso di S. E., Federzoni," *Il Giornale d'Italia*, May 17, 1936, 1. See also Fernando Mezzasoma, "Arte del tempo fascista," *Universalità fascista* (March, 1937): 247; "Il partito e la rivoluzione," *Universalità fascista* (January, 1932) 4; Cesare Colliva, "Volontarismo," *Meridiani* (August, 1935): 5; "Il duce e l'impero," *Il Giornale d'Italia*, May 13, 1936, 1.

55. Adolf Hitler, *Mein Kampf* (New York: Mariner, 1999), 290.

56. Ivon De Begnac, *Vita di Benito Mussolini* (Milan: Mondadori, 1940), 551.

57. For my own interpretation of this dimension of fascism, see Federico Finchelstein, *From Fascism to Populism in History* (Oakland: University of California Press, 2017). See also Benjamin Zachariah, "A Voluntary Gleichschaltung?: Indian Perspectives Towards a Non-Eurocentric Understanding of Fascism," *Transcultural Studies* 2 (2014): 82; Aristotle Kallis, "Transnational Fascism: The Fascist New Order, Violence, and Creative Destruction," in *Fascism Without Borders: Transnational Connections and Cooperation Between Movements and Regimes in Europe, 1918–1945*, ed. Arnd Bauerkämper, Grzegorz Rossoliński-Liebe (New York: Berghahn, 2017), 39–64; Ángel Alcalde, *War Veterans and Fascism in Interwar Europe* (Cambridge: Cambridge University Press, 2017); Andrea Mammone, *Transnational Neo-Fascism in France and Italy* (Cambridge: Cambridge University Press, 2015); Matteo Albanese and Pablo del Hierro, *Transnational Fascism in the Twentieth Century: Spain, Italy and the Global Neo-Fascist Network* (London: Bloomsbury, 2016). On the immediacy of the notion of empire, see Ann Laura Stoler, "Intimidations of Empire: Predicaments of the Tactile and the Unseen," in *Haunted by Empire: Geographies of Intimacy in North American History*, ed. Ann Laura Stoler (Durham: Duke University Press, 2006).

58. See, for example, letter to Ernst Freud, February 20, 1934, in Freud, *The Letters of Sigmund Freud*, 420; letters to Ernest Jones, July 23, 1933, and October 15, 1933, in Paskauskas, *The Complete Correspondence of Sigmund Freud and Ernest Jones*, 725, 731.

59. "This underarticulation, indeed the suspicion of articulation, functions as well as a critique of ideology. In the context of the baroque regimes of representation, it functions as well as a critique of representation." Steinberg, *Judaism Musical and Unmusical*.

60. See letter to Ernst Freud, January 17, 1937, in Freud, *The Letters of Sigmund Freud*, 440. Freud also wrote one year later that the Jewish people "owes its tenacity in supporting life to him, however, also much of the hostility which it has met and is meeting still." He opposed this support of life to "brutality and the inclination to violence." Freud, *Moses and Monotheism*, 136, 147.

61. Freud, *Moses and Monotheism*, 6. See also Sigmund Freud, *The Psychopathology of Everyday Life* (New York: Norton, 1965 [1901]), 84; Sigmund Freud, *Group Psychology and the Analysis of the Ego* (New York: Norton, 1959 [1922]), 34–35.

62. Slavoj Žižek, *Did Somebody Say Totalitarianism?* (New York: Verso, 2001), 9. While it is true that this mythical engagement, as well as many others, are at the center of Freud's thought, this does not mean, as Jacques Rancière argues, that Freud established an "alliance" with the "old mythological heritage." Jacques Rancière, *The Aesthetic Unconscious* (Cambridge: Polity, 2001) 44.

63. Sigmund Freud, *Civilization and Its Discontents* (New York: Norton, 1962 [1930]), 44; Sigmund Freud, *The Question of Lay Analysis* (New York: Anchor, 1964 [1927]), 42–43; Sigmund Freud, *Introductory Lectures on Psychoanalysis* (New York: Norton, 1962 [1917]), 335. See also Freud "Why War?," 287.

64. On the Austrian Catholic context, see Steinberg, "The Catholic Culture of the Austrian Jews." On the Italian Catholic reaction to psychoanalysis, see D. Colombo, "Psychoanalysis and the Catholic Church in Italy: The Role of Father Agostino Gemelli, 1925–1953," *Journal of the History of the Behavioral Sciences* 39, no. 4 (2003): 333–48. See also See Michel David, *La psicoanalisi nella cultura italiana* (Turin: Boringhieri, 1970).

65. See Freud "Why War?," 284, 287.

66. Gramsci was himself often reticent about the theoretical possibilities opened by psychoanalysis; rather "psychoanalytically," he presented Freud's theories as a superstructural symptom of modern capitalist society in 1928. In 1931, Gramsci argued that Freud, like Cesare Lombroso,

wanted to build a "general philosophy" out of mere empirical observations. Later in 1935, Gramsci believed that psychoanalysis was a "science" that worked better with the upper classes and was not necessarily fit to study the subaltern classes. Nevertheless, Gramsci was highly receptive to Freud's interpretation of dreams and related the Freudian analysis of the Oedipus complex to a "new revolutionary ethics." See Antonio Gramsci, *Letteratura e vita nazionale* (Rome: Editori Riuniti, 1977); Gramsci, *Gli Intelletuali* (Rome: Editori Riuniti, 1977), 94; Gramsci, *Passato e presente* (Rome: Editori Riuniti, 1977), 284–285. In private matters, however, he was much more open to psychoanalysis, including his hopeful support of his wife's psychoanalytic treatment. See Aurelio Lepre, *Il Prigionero: Vita di Antonio Gramsci* (Rome-Bari: Laterza, 2000), 148–149; Gramsci, *Letters from Prison* (New York: Columbia University Press, 1994), 2:29. From his fascist jail Gramsci admitted: "Non ho potuto studiare le teorie di Freud." The fact that fascism victimized Gramsci, eventually promoting his death, left us without this needed study.

67. Freud, *Civilization and Its Discontents*, 41.
68. I borrow here from Louis Althusser's reading of the political implications of psychoanalysis: Althusser, *Machiavelli and Us* (London: Verso, 1999), 117,126. On the uncanny and antifascism, see Eli Zaretsky, "Beyond the Blues: Richard Wright, Psychoanalysis, and the Modern Idea of Culture," in *The Transnational Unconscious*, ed. Mariano Plotkin and Joy Damousi (London: Palgrave Macmillan, 2009).
69. See Giovacchino Forzano (with Benito Mussolini), *Campo di Maggio dramma in tre atti* (Florence: G. Barbèra, 1931). See also Giovacchino Forzano, *Mussolini: autore drammatico con facsimili di autografi inediti* (Florence: G. Barbèra, 1954); Roberto Zapperi, *Freud e Mussolini*, 11; Élisabeth Roudinesco, *Sigmund Freud: In His Time and Ours* (Cambridge, MA: Harvard University Press, 2016), 359.
70. Freud, *Group Psychology and the Analysis of the Ego*, 34–35.
71. Freud, *Civilization and Its Discontents*, 96, 112.
72. In his path-breaking analysis of this myth, the Italian psychoanalyst G. Contri, who was the first in analyzing and identifying it, argues that Freud's encrypted message to Mussolini was a sarcastic insult, namely, that he was a criminal. Contri's approach agrees with the traditional antifascist view that fascism was corrupt and dishonest. Inspired by Contri's insights on Freud and Prometheus, my reading is markedly different and stresses the relation between Freud's characterization of Mussolini as a "hero," the myth's relation to both the origins and the breaking down of culture and the mythological nature of fascism. In arguing against the

view that fascism is just barbarism, I connect the idea of barbarism to Freud's understanding of the unconscious nature of the limits to civilization as posed by the return of the repressed. See Giacomo B. Contri, *Lavoro dell'inconscio e lavoro psicoanalitico* (Milano: Sipiel, 1985), 90–93.

73. Sigmund Freud, "The Acquisition of Power Over Fire" (1932), in *Collected Papers* (London: Hogarth, 1957), 5:290–291.

74. Theodor Adorno, *Prisms* (Cambridge, MA: MIT Press, 1983), 247.

75. See Sigmund Freud, *The Future of an Illusion* (New York: Norton, 1961 [1927]), 6, 15. In this regard, Julia Kristeva argues: "The more or less beautiful image in which I behold or recognize myself rests upon an abjection that sunders it as soon as repression, the constant watchman, is relaxed." See Julia Kristeva, *Powers of Horror: An Essay on Abjection* (New York: Columbia University Press, 1982), 13. For Kristeva, abjection and abjecting represent a "precondition of narcissism."

76. See Sigmund Freud, *The "Wolfman" and Other Cases* (London: Penguin, 2003), 83. See also Karl Abraham, "Analysis of the Prometheus Saga," in *Dreams and Myths: A Study in Race Psychology* (New York: Journal of Nervous and Mental Diseases, 1913), 27.

77. Freud, *Group Psychology and the Analysis of the Ego*, 71. On the hero as appearing in history between the totem and the God, see Freud, *Moses and Monotheism*, 171.

78. As Gillian Rose perceptively notes, fascism abolishes the distinction between fantasy and political action. See Rose, *Mourning Becomes the Law: Philosophy and Representation* (Cambridge: Cambridge University Press, 1996), 53.

79. Freud, *Moses and Monotheism*, 139–140.

80. For Michael Steinberg: "The text's trajectory is complicated. Freud begun work on it in Vienna in 1934, published its first two sections in *Imago* in 1937, and continued to work on it in exile in London in the second half of 1938. The German text was published in Amsterdam in 1939." Steinberg argues that the book presents two subject positions, namely, the preexile and postexile voices. "The pre-exile argument claims to take Moses away from the Jews. It destabilizes Jewish historical paternity. The post-exile voice claims the position of a new father. In exile, Freud is Moses—a new Moses. Here is the problem: does exile work through the problem of an excessive identification with the super-ego, with the replacement of the father? In other words, does Freud take on the voice of Moses only from the vantage point of exile, so that Freud's Moses—Freud as Moses—assumes the mantle of the father without fulfilling the mortal contract between primal father and son? Replacing the father in the primal contract requires

patricide. Exile, however, may literally shift the grounds of succession adequately to provide an escape from the primal contract and from the bounds of patricide." See Steinberg, *Judaism Musical and Unmusical*, chap. 2. See also Eric Santner, *On the Psychotheology of Everyday Life: Reflections on Freud and Rosenzweig* (Chicago: University of Chicago Press, 2001), 7.

81. Gay, *Freud: A Life for Our Time*, 595.

82. Letter to Ernst Freud, February 20, 1934, in Freud, *The Letters of Sigmund Freud*, 419.

83. Freud, *Group Psychology and the Analysis of the Ego*, 88–89.

84. Jones, *The Life and Work of Sigmund Freud*, 3:181, 219.

85. Freud told Jones in 1934: "Perhaps at this very moment the intriguer M. in Venice is selling us to the captain of the thieves H." Letter to Ernest Jones, June 16, 1934, in Paskauskas, *The Complete Correspondence of Sigmund Freud and Ernest Jones*, 737.

86. On the notion of the negative sublime and fascism, see Dominick LaCapra, *History and Memory After Auschwitz* (Ithaca: Cornell University Press, 1998), 27–30; LaCapra, *Representing the Holocaust: History, Theory, Trauma* (Ithaca, NY: Cornell University Press, 1994), 100–110; and LaCapra, *Writing History, Writing Trauma*, 94.

87. Mussolini opposed fascist relativism to "scientificism." See Benito Mussolini, *Diuturna* (Milano: Imperia, 1924), 375. Many antifascists, such as Piero Gobetti, noted the centrality of Mussolini's relativism. See Piero Gobetti, "Benito Mussolini," in *On Liberal Revolution* (New Haven, CT: Yale University Press, 2000) p. 58. It is interesting to note that Hannah Arendt was equally interested in this aspect of Mussolini's ideology and connected it with the Romantic tradition. Arendt, *The Origins of Totalitarianism*, 168. Sigmund Freud, *New Introductory Lectures on Psychoanalysis* (New York: Norton, 1965 [1933]), 175–176.

88. Freud, *Moses and Monotheism*, 67.

89. I want to thank Eli Zaretsky for sharing with me his interpretation of Freud's notion of communism as the historical return of the band of brothers that had killed the father.

90. Freud, *Moses and Monotheism*, 96.

91. Jones, *The Life and Work of Sigmund Freud*, 3:189.

92. See Freud "Why War?," 277.

93. Freud, 278.

94. Letter to Ernest Jones, March 2, 1937, in Paskauskas, *The Complete Correspondence of Sigmund Freud and Ernest Jones*, 757.

95. Letter to George Sylvester Viereck, July 20, 1928, in Freud, *The Letters of Sigmund Freud*, 381.

96. Sander Gilman, *Love + Marriage= Death, and Other Essays on Represent-ing Difference* (Stanford: Stanford University Press, 1998), 58.
97. In the same paragraph, and without noticing the change, Freud goes on to describe the fundamental aspect of Judaism, namely, its constitutive challenge to oppression. Freud, *Moses and Monotheism*, 115–116. On Freud's relation vis-à-vis Eastern Jews, see Sander Gilman, *Freud, Race and Gen-der* (Princeton: Princeton University Press, 1993).
98. Freud argues: "the gratification of these destructive impulses is of course facilitated by their admixture with others of an erotic and idealistic kind." See Freud, "Why War?," 282.
99. On the fascist theory of the abject, see Federico Finchelstein, "On Fascist Ideology," *Constellations: An International Journal of Critical and Demo-cratic Theory* 15, no. 3 (2008): 320–331.

3. Borges and Fascism as Mythology

1. "¿No ha razonado Freud y no ha presentido Walt Whitman que los hom-bres gozan de poca información acerca de los móviles profundos de su con-ducta?" Borges, "Anotación al 23 de Agosto de 1944," in *Obras Completas* (Barcelona: Emecé, 1996), 2:106.
2. Borges, 2:106.
3. Borges's connection with psychoanalysis was intensely ambiguous. In 1937, for example, he referred to the theories of Freud as "aniquilables." Borges, *Obras Completas*, 4:329. See also page 380. Borges admitted reading Freud and said he was disappointed. He actually presented him as mentally unstable and presented his theories as pansexualism. "I think of him [Freud] as a kind of madman, no? A man laboring over a sexual obsession. Well, perhaps he didn't take it to heart. Perhaps he was just doing it as a kind of game." Borges contrasted Freud to Jung and praised the latter for creating a mythology. In contrast, "in the case of Freud, it all boils down to a few rather unpleasant facts. But, of course, that's merely my ignorance or my bias." Richard Burgin, *Conversations with Jorge Luis Borges* (New York: Holt, Rinehart and Winston, 1969), 109. Nonetheless, Borges undertook psychoanalytic sessions with a psycho-analyst in 1945 and again with another psychoanalyst in 1950. See Edwin Williamson, *Borges: A Life* (London: Penguin, 2004), 287–290, 315; and Rita Goldaracena, "Las inhibiciones del joven Borges," *El País* (Madrid), December 23, 1990.
4. Borges, "Anotación al 23 de Agosto de 1944," in *Obras Completas*, 2:105.

5. In his "Definition of the Germanophile" of 1940, Borges summarized a "conversación que he tenido con muchos germanófilos, y en la que juro no volver a incurrir, porque el tiempo otorgado a los mortales no es infinito y el fruto de esas conferencias es vano." Borges, "Definición del Germanófilo," in *Obras Completas*, 4:442. In 1945, Borges identified Communism, Nazism, Surrealism, and even psychoanalysis as symptoms of an era that was "bajamente romántica" and "melancólica." See Borges, *Obras Completas*, 2:65. Sergio Pastormerlo notes that in this passage Borges emphasizes the political dimension of the Romantic phenomenon that he understood as a collection of different forms of hatred. See Sergio Pastormerlo, *Borges Crítico* (Buenos Aires: Fondo de Cultura Económica, 2007), 112–113. It is important to note that, in that instance, the Borgean collection of hated objects (namely, Nazism, Communism, Surrealism, and psychoanalysis) eliminated nuances and reproduced the perceived dimension of the criticized phenomena as Borges frequently expressed it in his private conversations with Bioy Casares. In these talks, in 1958 Borges identified "the Freudian" with denial and the unconscious, that is, with the possibility of making an interpretation of what is implicit (423). One year later he complains to Bioy: "Ya Freud es considerado como la verdad" (602). See Adolfo Bioy Casares, *Borges* (Buenos Aires: Destino, 2006).

6. Borges, "Definición del Germanófilo," 4:442; Borges, "Ensayo de imparcialidad," *Sur* 61 (October 1939): 27.

7. "Es de naturaleza moral, y es casi increíble": Borges "Definición del Germanófilo," 4:442. See also page 338. On the origins of the discussion on means and ends, see page 341. For an excellent discussion of the place of ethics in the Borgean interpretation of Nazism, see Annick Louis, *Borges ante el fascismo* (Frankfurt: Peter Lang, 2007), 284. In a previous text, Louis argues that "Borges's militancy against fascism is pathetic" ("la militancia de Borges contra el nazismo resulta patética"); see her article "Borges y el nazismo," *Variaciones Borges* 4 (1997). Louis presents Borges as willing to transform reality into fictional material. She also thinks that Borges often had a "precarious" conception of Nazism. Without denying this Borgean displacement from reality to fiction—a displacement that mirrors the efforts of some of the characters in his wartime stories, as we will see is the case with Jaromir Hladik or even David Jerusalem—my intention in this chapter is to argue the opposite view. In other words, I here highlight how the historical and interpretative dimension of the Borgean wartime storytelling, as well as his nonfictional political writing, offers a critical theory of fascism. I have previously addressed some of these issues in a preliminary manner in Federico Finchelstein, "Borges, la Shoah

y el 'Mensaje kafkiano': un ensayo de interpretación," *Espacios de Crítica y Producción: Publicación de la Facultad de Filosofía y Letras-Universidad de Buenos Aires* 25 (1999). Other works on Borges also explore this relation between Borges and Nazism: among them see especially those of Aizenberg, Senkman, and Stavans: Edna Aizenberg, *Borges, el tejedor del Aleph y otros ensayos* (Frankfurt: Vervuert: 1997); Leonardo Senkman, "Borges y el mal del nazismo," in *Borges en Jerusalén*, ed. Myrna Solotorevsky and Ruth Fine (Frankfurt: Vervuert, 2003); Ilan Stavans, "A Comment on Borges's Response to Hitler," *Modern Judaism* 23, no. 1 (2003); Leonardo Senkman and Saul Sosnowski, *Fascismo y nazismo en las letras argentinas* (Buenos Aires: Lumiere, 2009), 87–89.

8. Borges, "Definición del Germanófilo," 4:442, and see also page 427.

9. "Adolf Hitler obra a lo Zarathustra, más allá del bien y del mal." Jorge Luis Borges, "Ensayo de imparcialidad," *Sur* 61 (October 1939): 27.

10. Jacques Lacan, *The Four Fundamental Concepts of Psycho-Analysis* (New York: Norton, 1981), 275.

11. In Agamben's view, traumatic experience seems to illuminate the analytic sense of things. In short, he endows the sacrificed victim with authentic knowledge about the world. The language of authenticity works as a legitimizing device for victims, and for Agamben as their interpreter. They comprehend the world in ways that escape nonvictims. See Giorgio Agamben, *Remnants of Auschwitz: The Witness and the Archive* (New York: Zone, 1999). For criticisms of Agamben in this regard, see Dominick LaCapra, *History in Transit: Experience, Identity, Critical Theory* (Ithaca, NY: Cornell University Press, 2004), chap. 4; and María Pía Lara, *Narrating Evil: A Postmetaphysical Theory of Reflective Judgment* (New York: Columbia University Press, 2007).

12. Berel Lang, "The Representation of Limits," in *Probing the Limits of Representation*, ed. Saul Friedlander (Cambridge, MA: Harvard University Press, 1992). See also Berel Lang, *Holocaust Representation: Art Within the Limits of History and Ethics* (Baltimore: Johns Hopkins University Press, 2000); and Lang, *Philosophical Witnessing: The Holocaust as Presence* (Waltham, MA: University Press of New England, 2009).

13. George Steiner, "Los libros no tienen prisa," *Letra Internacional* 45 (1996): 39. On the experience of the survivors and suicide, see also Amos Goldberg, "Holocaust Diaries as 'Life Stories,' " *Search and Research* 5, Yad Vashem (2004). Agnes Heller refers to this impossibility apropos of Adorno's famous remark: "Can poetry be written after Auschwitz? Or rather, can poetry be written about Auschwitz? No, nothing can be written about Auschwitz. But yes. One can write about all the silences surrounding

Auschwitz: the silence of guilt, of shame, of horror, and of senselessness. One can open up these silences. One not only can. One should write about Auschwitz, about the Holocaust." Agnes Heller and Ferenc Fehér, *The Grandeur and Twilight of Radical Universalism* (New Brunswick, NJ: Transaction, 1991), 400.

14. The third description of the battle, implausibly, is encompassed by one line, which inexorably is the last one. The story ends: "Del poeta sabemos que se dio muerte al salir del palacio; del rey que es un mendigo que recorre los caminos de Irlanda, que fue su reino, y que no ha repetido nunca el poema." Borges, *Obras Completas*, 3:47. This story is perceptively analyzed by Roger Chartier, *Pluma de ganso, libro de letras y oro viajero* (México: Universidad Iberoamericana, 1997), 13–19. Referring to the impossibility of communication in Borges, Bruno Bosteels observes, "There seems to be, then, a dimension of reality, or perhaps it would be better to say a dimension of the real—whether cruel or not—that forever remains beyond the scope of language." See Bruno Bosteels, "Borges as Antiphilosopher," in *Thinking With Borges*, ed. William Egginton and David E. Johnson (Aurora, CO: David Group, 2009).

15. I will return to this story in the conclusion of this book.

16. Borges, "Definición del Germanófilo," 4:441–443; and see also "Dos poetas politicos," 427.

17. Elie Wiesel, "Some Questions That Remain Open," in *Comprehending the Holocaust: Historical and Literary Research*, ed. Asher Cohen, Joav Gelber, and Charlotte Wardi (Frankfurt am Main: Peter Lang, 1988), 117.

18. Franz Kafka, *Relatos Completos I* (Buenos Aires: Losada, 1994), 124. This is the edition translated by Borges in 1938. Borges later claimed in 1970 that, although he appeared in 1938 as the sole translator of this book of Kafka's stories, he translated all stories with the exception of "The Metamorphosis."

19. See George Steiner, "The Long Life Metaphor: A Theological-Metaphysical Approach to the Shoah," in Cohen, Gelber, Charlotte Wardi, *Comprehending the Holocaust*, 58.

20. See Primo Levi, *Si esto es un Hombre* (Buenos Aires: Milá, 1988), 31.

21. Franz Kafka, *Relatos Completos I*, 125. In the translation by Borges: "Hallábase, a ser posible, aún más firmemente convencido de que tenía que desaparecer."

22. "Nos hemos acostumbrado a recibir bofetadas sin ninguna razón, a los golpes, a las ejecuciones. Nos hemos acostumbrado a ver morir a la gente en sus propios excrementos, a ver los féretros con su carga y montones de cadáveres; a ver cómo los enfermos se revuelcan en la mugre y a ver la

desesperada impotencia de los médicos. Nos hemos acostumbrado a que de vez en cuando lleguen por aquí mil infelices y a que otros mil partan de tanto en tanto." Petr Fischl, "Nos hemos acostumbrado," in *Aquí no vuelan las mariposas: Poemas y dibujos infantiles: terezin, 1942–1944* (Buenos Aires: Milá, 1988), 17.

23. Norbert Elias, "Notes sur les juifs en tant que participant á une relation établis-marginaux," in *Norbert Elias par lui-même* (Paris: Agora, 1991).

24. Saul Friedlander, "Some Aspects of the Historical Significance of the Holocaust," *Jerusalem Quarterly* 1 (1976). See also Saul Friedlander, *Nazi Germany and the Jews: The Years of Persecution, 1933–1939* (New York: Harper Perennial, 1998); and Friedlander, *The Years of Extermination* (New York: Harper, 2007). For a critical analysis of Friedlander's interpretation of the victims' perspective, see Amos Goldberg, "The Victim's Voice and Melodramatic Aesthetics in History," *History and Theory* 48, no. 3 (October 2009).

25. See Borges, *Obras Completas*, 4:306, 326; 2:31. The *degüello* metaphor is highly meaningful for Borges. He places this practice within the trope of generic barbarism. Almost without establishing contextual differences, Borges conflates victims and times on both sides of the Atlantic. Years later, he would link the fate of the victims of the nineteenth-century Argentine barbarism denounced by Sarmiento to the victimization of Anne Frank. To a great extent, Borges conflated fascism in general with Argentine fascism and its vindicated genealogy (Rosas). Jorge Luis Borges, *The Aleph, and Other Stories* (New York: Dutton, 1970), 206; Borges, "Pedro Salvadores," in *Obras Completas*, 2:372–373.

26. See Jorge Luis Borges, prologue to Domingo Faustino Sarmiento, *Recuerdos de provincia* (Buenos Aires: Emece Editores, 1944). On the topic of civilization and barbarism in Borges, see Daniel Balderston, *¿Fuera de contexto?: Referencialidad histórica y expresión de la realidad en Borges* (Rosario: Beatriz Viterbo Editora, 1996), 131–157. On this topic, see also Doris Sommer, *Foundational Fictions: The National Romances of Latin America* (Berkeley: University of California Press, 1991).

27. Sommer, *Foundational Fictions*.

28. "En muchos casos, el conocimiento de que ciertas felicidades eran simple fábrica del azar, hubiera aminorado su virtud; para eludir ese inconveniente, los agentes de la Compañía usaban de las sugestiones y de la magia. Sus pasos, sus manejos, eran secretos. Para indagar las íntimas esperanzas y los íntimos terrores de cada cual, disponían de astrólogos y de espías. Había ciertos leones de piedra, había una letrina sagrada llamada Qaphqa." Cited in Beatriz Sarlo, *Borges, un escritor en las orillas*

(Buenos Aires: Ariel, 1998), 173. On Borges and Kafka, see also Juan De Castro, *The Spaces of Latin American Literature: Tradition, Globalization and Cultural Production* (New York: Palgrave Macmillan, 2008), 55–57. See Borges, *Obras Completas*, 1:458; in English, see Jorge Luis Borges, *Labyrinths* (New York: New Directions, 1964), 33. On the historiographical tendency to emphasize the role of Nazi bureaucracy in the Holocaust while at the same time downplaying the role of ideology, see Federico Finchelstein, "The Holocaust Canon: Rereading Raul Hilberg," *New German Critique* 96 (Fall 2005). On Borges and his emphasis on fascism and technology, see Borges, "Wells previsor," *Sur* 26 (November 1936): 126. Borges argues: "la ocupación tiránica de Abisinia [Ethiopia] fue obra de los aviadores y de los *chauffeurs* -y del temor, tal vez un poco mitológico, de los perversos laboratorios de Hitler."

29. See Jorge Luís Borges, "Nathaniel Hawthorne" (1949), in *Obras Completas*, 2:55; Borges, "Franz Kafka," in *Obras Completas*, 4:454.

30. Jorge Luis Borges, "Anotación al 23 de Agosto de 1944," in *Obras Completas*, 2:105–106.

31. "Las interjecciones han usurpado la función de los razonamientos; es verdad que los atolondrados que las emiten, distraídamente les dan un aire discursivo y que ese tenue simulacro sintáctico satisface y persuade a quienes los oyen. El que ha jurado que la guerra es una especie de *yijad* liberal contra las dictaduras, acto continuo anhela que Mussolini milite contra Hitler: operación que aniquilaría su tesis." Jorge Luis Borges, "Ensayo de imparcialidad," *Sur* 61 (October 1939): 27.

32. "Wells, increíblemente, no es nazi. Increíblemente, pues casi todos mis contemporáneos lo son, aunque lo nieguen o ignoren. Desde 1925, no hay publicista que no opine que el hecho inevitable y trivial de haber nacido en un determinado país y de pertenecer a tal raza (o a tal buena mixtura de razas) no sea un privilegio singular y un talismán suficiente." Borges, *Obras Completas*, 2:101–102.

33. "Vindicadores de la democracia, que se creen muy distintos de Goebbels, instan a sus lectores, en el dialecto mismo del enemigo, a escuchar los latidos de un corazón que recoge los íntimos mandatos de la sangre y de la tierra." See Borges, *Obras Completas*, 2:101–102. It is interesting to note that Borges presents the year 1925, that is, the year fascism becomes clearly dictatorial, as the moment when extreme nationalism becomes a global opinion.

34. See Vittorino Vezzani, "Gli ideali di vita del fascismo" *Gerarchia* (December 1934): 1011.

35. "Mussolini dichiara 'fondamentale' la dottrina di Rocco," *Il Giornale d'Italia*, September 2, 1925.

36. See, for example, Volt, "L'Illusione conservatrice," *Critica Fascista* (March 1, 1925): 82.

37. Giuseppe Bottai, "La forza di Mussolini," *Critica Fascista* (April 1, 1934): 122.

38. Asvero Gravelli, "Chi si ferma è perduto," *Gerarchia* (July 1938) 466. On the leader as a hero vis-à-vis the masses, see also Ernesto Gimenez Caballero, "I Fascisti spagnuoli," *Gerarchia* (February 1934): 110–123.

39. Margherita G. Sarfatti, "Individualismo e fascismo," *Gerarchia* (March 1931): 223–228.

40. See Camillo Pellizzi, "L'iniziativa individuale nella politica fascista," *Gerarchia* (December 1931): 995–998. See also Libero Merlino, "Fascismo, libertà, fuoriuscitismo," *Gerarchia* (January 1930) 14–19.

41. See Simonetta Falasca-Zamponi, "Fascism and Aesthetics," *Constellations* 15, no. 3 (2008).

42. Beatriz Sarlo, *Borges, Un escritor en las orillas* (Buenos Aires: Ariel, 1998), 191.

43. "El verdadero intelectual rehúya los debates contemporáneos: la realidad es siempre anacrónica." Borges, *Obras Completas*, 2:103.

44. Borges commented that Russell argued that "in a sense" there was a dichotomy between the rationality of the early eighteenth century and the irrationality of "our time." Borges adds: "I would eliminate the timid adverb that starts the sentence" ("Yo eliminaría el tímido adverbio que encabeza la frase"). Borges, 2:104.

45. "Seré fusilado por torturador y asesino. El tribunal ha procedido con rectitud; desde el principio yo me he declarado culpable. Mañana cuando el reloj dé la prisión de las nueve, yo habré entrado en la muerte." Borges, *Obras Completas*, 1:576; Borges, *Labyrinths*, 141.

46. Years later, in 1969, Borges would add that Zur Linde represents a Platonic idea of the Nazi. See Luz Rodriguez Carranza, "Réquiem para un fin de siglo," *Anthropos* 142–143 (1993): 89.

47. "Ya que a pesar de no carecer de valor, me faltaba toda vocación de violencia. Comprendí, sin embargo que estábamos al borde de un tiempo nuevo y que ese tiempo comparable a las épocas iniciales del Islam o del Cristianismo, exigía hombre nuevos. Individualmente mis camaradas me eran odiosos; en vano procuré razonar que para el alto fin que nos congregaba no éramos individuos." Borges, *Obras Completas*, 1:577; Borges, *Labyrinths*, 142–143.

48. "El nazismo intrínsecamente, es un hecho moral, un despojarse del viejo hombre, para vestir el nuevo. En la batalla esa mutación es común, entre el clamor de los capitanes y el vocerío; no así en un torpe calabozo, donde nos tienta con antiguas ternuras la insidiosa piedad. No en vano

3. BORGES AND FASCISM AS MYTHOLOGY

escribo esa palabra; la piedad por el hombre nuevo es el último pecado de Zarathustra. Casi lo cometí (lo confieso) cuando nos remitieron de Breslau al insigne poeta David Jerusalem." Borges, *Obras Completas*, 1:578.

49. Jorge Luis Borges, "Letras Alemanas: Una exposición afligente," *Sur 8*, no. 49 (1938): 67. See also Borges, "Definición del Germanófilo," 4:441. In this regard, Borges remains within the sphere of Argentine antifascism in particular, and of global antifascist culture in general. See the introduction and second chapter in Federico Finchelstein, *Transatlantic Fascism: Ideology, Violence, and the Sacred in Argentina and Italy, 1919–1945* (Durham: Duke University Press, 2010). On antifascism, see Andrés Bisso, *Acción Argentina: un antifascismo nacional en tiempos de guerra mundial* (Buenos Aires: Prometeo, 2005); and Bisso, *El antifascismo argentino* (Buenos Aires: CeDInCI Editores, 2007). On Borges and the literary milieu of Argentine antifascism, see John King, *Sur: A Study of the Argentine Literary Journal and Its Role in the Development of a Culture, 1931–1970* (Cambridge: Cambridge University Press, 1986); and Rosalie Sitman, "Protest from Afar: The Jewish and Republican Presence in Victoria Ocampo's Revista SUR in the 1930s and 1940s," in *Rethinking Jewish-Latin Americans*, ed. Jeffrey Lesser and Raanan Rein (Albuquerque: University of New Mexico Press, 2008).

50. On the different concepts of *Bildung* for victims and perpetrators, see George Mosse, *German Jews Beyond Judaism* (Bloomington: Indiana University Press, 1985).

51. Dominick LaCapra, preface to Federico Finchelstein, ed., *Los Alemanes, el Holocausto y la Culpa Colectiva: el Debate Goldhagen* (Buenos Aires: Eudeba, 1999), 24; Dominick LaCapra, *Writing History, Writing Trauma* (Baltimore: Johns Hopkins University Press, 2001), 133.

52. "Yo agonicé con él, yo morí con él, yo de algún modo me he perdido con él; por eso, fui implacable." Borges, *Obras Completas*, 1:579; Borges, *Labyrinths*, 145.

53. Max Horkheimer and Theodor Adorno, *Dialectic of Enlightenment* (Stanford: Stanford University Press, 2002). For an earlier take on the mythological lack of distinction between subjects and objects, see Jorge Luis Borges, *Textos Recobrados 1919–1929* (Buenos Aires: Emecé, 1997), 262. In this text from 1926, Borges thinks about this dimension specifically but not exclusively for the case of Mexico.

54. "Fui severo con él, no permití que me ablandaran ni la compasión ni su gloria. Yo había comprendido que no hay cosa en el mundo que no sea germen de un infierno posible; un rostro, una palabra una brújula, un aviso de cigarrillos, podrían enloquecer a una persona, si ésta no lograra

olvidarlos. ¿No estaría loco un hombre que continuamente se figurara el mapa de Hungría? Determiné aplicar ese principio al régimen disciplinario de nuestra casa y . . . a fines de 1942, Jerusalem perdió la razón; el primero de marzo de 1942, logró darse muerte." Borges, *Obras Completas*, 1:579; Borges, *Labyrinths*, 145.

55. "Ha sido inevitable aquí omitir unas líneas": Borges, *Obras Completas*, 1:579; Borges, *Labyrinths*, 145.

4. Borges and the Persistence of Myth

1. Borges, *Obras Completas* (Barcelona: Emecé, 1996), 1:508; Jorge Luis Borges, *Labyrinths* (New York: New Directions, 1964), 89.

2. The analysis of this story is clearly relevant for the late-nineteenth-century Argentine historiography concerned with the construction of a national pantheon. The involvement of a European Jewish refugee in such a fundamentally *criollo* and nationalistic topic is, in my view, an intentional irony by Borges. Indeed, he is personally attracted to heroes, but, on a more conceptual level, he is also ashamed of the superficiality of the exchange between two men he deems vain (Bolívar and San Martín), which he then attempts to frame as the corollary of a philosophy (Schopenhauer's). It would seem, then, that the historian from Prague does not believe in the literality of texts and, contrary to his perhaps more naive Argentine-born counterpart, the Jewish historian prefers a method based on clues and insights and is highly suspicious of the intentions behind conventional primary sources.

3. On the subject position of exile of Enzo Traverso, *La pensée dispersée: figures de l'exil judéo-allemand* (Paris: Léo Scheer, 2004). See also the classic text by Hannah Arendt, "Between Pariah and Parvenu," in *The Origins of Totalitarianism* (New York: Meridian, 1959), 56–68. On the subject of immigration, Diaspora, and Argentine Jewish identity, see Raanan Rein, *Argentine Jews or Jewish Argentines?: Essays on History, Ethnicity and Diaspora* (Boston: Brill, 2010).

4. "Usted es el genuino historiador. Su gente anduvo por los campos de América y libró las grandes batallas, mientras la mía, oscura, apenas emergía del *ghetto*. Usted lleva la historia en la sangre, según sus elocuentes palabras; a usted le basta oír con atención esa voz recóndita. Yo, en cambio, debo transferirme a Sulaco y descifrar papeles y papeles acaso apócrifos." Borges, *Obras Completas*, 2:441.

5. "De su labor, sin duda benemérita, sólo he podido examinar una vindicación de la república semítica de Cartago, que la posteridad juzga a

través de los historiadores romanos, sus enemigos, y una suerte de ensayo que sostiene que el gobierno no debe ser una función visible y patética." Borges, *Obras Completas*, 2:439.

6. "Este alegato mereció la refutación decisiva de Martín Heidegger, que demostró, mediante fotocopias de los titulares de los periódicos, que el moderno jefe de estado, lejos de ser anónimo, es más bien el protagonista, el corega, el David danzante, que mima el drama de su pueblo, asistido de pompa escénica y recurriendo, sin vacilar, a las hipérboles del arte oratorio. Probó asimismo que el linaje de Zimmermann era hebreo, por no decir judío. Esta publicación del venerado existencialista fue la inmediata causa del éxodo y de las trashumantes actividades de nuestro huésped." Borges, *Obras Completas*, 2:439.

7. "¿Quién no jugó a los antepasados alguna vez, a las prehistorias de su carne y su sangre? Yo lo hago muchas veces, y muchas no me disgustó pensarme judío. Se trata de una hipótesis haragana, de una aventura sedentaria y frugal que a nadie perjudica- ni siquiera a la fama de Israel, ya que mi judaísmo era sin palabras, como las canciones de Mendelssohn." Jorge Luis Borges, "Yo, Judío," *Megáfono* 3, no. 12 (April 1934): 2. The accusation published in *Crisol* would recur, for instance, in "La 'Prensa' Judaizada," *Nuevo Orden*, April 30, 1941, 11.

8. "*Crisol*, en su numero del 30 de enero, ha querido halagar esa retrospectiva esperanza y habla de mi 'ascendencia judía, maliciosamente ocultada' (El participio y el adverbio me maravillan)." Borges, "Yo, Judío," 2.

9. "Borges Acevedo es mi nombre. Ramos Mejía, en cierta nota del capítulo quinto de *Rosas y su tiempo*, enumera los apellidos porteños de aquella fecha, para demostrar que todos, o casi todos, 'procedían de cepa hebreoportuguesa.' Acevedo figura en ese catalogo: único documento de mis pretensiones judías, hasta la confirmación de *Crisol*. Sin embargo, el capitán Honorio Acevedo ha realizado investigaciones precisas que no puedo ignorar. Ellas me indican el primer Acevedo que desembarcó en esta tierra, el catalán don Pedro de Acevedo, maestre de campo, ya poblador del 'Pago de los Arroyos' en 1728, padre y antepasado de estancieros de esta provincia, varón de quien informan los *Anales del Rosario de Santa Fe* y los *Documentos para la historia del Virreinato*-abuelo, en fin, casi irreparablemente español. Doscientos años y no doy con el israelita, doscientos años y el antepasado me elude." Borges, 2.

10. "Como los drusos, como la luna, como la muerte, como la semana que viene, el pasado remoto es de aquellas cosas que puede enriquecer la ignorancia-que se alimentan sobre todo de la ignorancia. Es infinitamente plástico y agradable, mucho más servicial que el porvenir y mucho menos

exigente de esfuerzos. Es la estación famosa predilecta de los mitologías." Borges, 2.

11. Borges, 2.

12. On several occasions, Borges took part in antifascist campaigns against anti-Semitism. He also sporadically held anti-Semitic positions in private conversations. While he was not Jewish, he wrote stories with Jewish narrators and used Jewish identity as a subject position for interpretation. Regarding Borges's activities in the antifascist campaigns against anti-Semitism, see IWO Archive, Buenos Aires, Argentina, Caja Organización Popular contra el Antisemitismo, Correspondencia Panfletos, Publicaciones C, 1936–1937 C, 1939.

13. "La diferencia entre judíos y no judíos me parece, en general, insignificante; a veces ilusoria o imperceptible." Borges, *Obras Completas*, 2:102.

14. "A mí personalmente me indigna, menos por Israel que por Alemania, menos por la injuriada comunidad que por la injuriosa nación. No se si el mundo puede prescindir de la civilización alemana." Jorge Luis Borges, "Una pedagogía del odio," *Sur* 32 (May 1937): 81.

15. Jorge Luis Borges, "Ensayo de imparcialidad," *Sur* 61 (October 1939): 28. On Borges and cosmopolitanism, see the excellent work of Mariano Siskind, "El cosmopolitismo como problema político: Borges y el desafío de la modernidad," *Variaciones Borges* 24 (2007): 75–92.

16. "Ciertos desagradecidos católicos—léase personas afiliadas a la Iglesia de Roma, que es una secta disidente israelita servida por un personal italiano, que atiende al público los días feriados y domingos—quieren introducir en esta plaza una tenebrosa doctrina, de confesado origen alemán, rutenio, ruso, polonés, valaco y moldavo." *Mundo Israelita*, August 20, 1932, 1.

17. "Basta la sola enunciación de ese rosario lóbrego para que el alarmado argentino pueda apreciar toda la gravedad del complot. Por cierto que se trata de un producto más deletéreo y mucho menos gratuito que el DUMPING. Se trata—soltemos de una vez la palabra obscena del Antisemitismo." See *Mundo Israelita*, August 20, 1932, 1. Borges calls attention to the possibility of the repetition of the anti-Semitic pogrom of 1919 in Argentina: "Borrajeo con evidente prisa esta nota. En ella no quiero omitir, sin embargo, que instigar odios me parece una tristísima actividad y que hay proyectos edilicios mejores que la delicada reconstrucción, balazo a balazo, de nuestra Semana de Enero—aunque nos quieran sobornar con la vista de la enrojecida calle Junín, hecha una sola llama." On the history of Argentine anti-Semitism, see Leonardo Senkman, ed., *El antisemitismo en la Argentina* (Buenos Aires: Ceal, 1989); Daniel Lvovich, *Nacionalismo y antisemitismo en la Argentina* (Buenos Aires: Ed. Vergara, 2003); and

Lvovich, "Una intervención de Borges contra el antisemitismo," *Nuestra Memoria* 22 (2003). See also Federico Finchelstein, *The Ideological Origins of the Dirty War: Fascism, Populism, and Dictatorship in Twentieth Century Argentina* (Oxford: Oxford University Press, 2014), chap. 3.

18. "Quienes recomiendan su empleo, suelen culpar a los judíos, a todos, de la crucifixión de Jesús. Olvidan que su propia fe ha declarado que la cruz operó nuestra redención. Olvidan que inculpar a los judíos equivale a inculpar a los vertebrados, o aún a los mamíferos." *Mundo Israelita*, August 20, 1932, 1.

19. "Olvidan que cuando Jesucristo quiso ser hombre, prefirió ser judío, y que NO eligió ser francés ni siquiera porteño, ni vivir en el año 1932 después de Jesucristo para suscribirse por un año a LE ROSEAU DE'OR. Olvidan que Jesús, ciertamente, no fue un judío converso. La basílica de Luján, para Él, hubiera sido tan indescifrable espectáculo como un calentador a gas o un antisemita." *Mundo Israelita*, August 20, 1932, 1.

20. "Soy un pobre cristiano. . . . Llévese todos esos mamotretos, si quiere; no tengo tiempo que perder en supersticiones judías." Borges, *Obras Completas*, 1:500; Borges, *Labyrinths*, 79. In her suggestive analysis, Louis notes that the Argentine fascist publications presented in the story (*La Cruz de la Espada* and *El Mártir*, edited by Ernst Palast-Ernesto Palacio) contrast what is Jewish to what is Christian and define the events as a "pogrom clandestino y frugal." See Annick Louis, *Borges ante el fascismo* (Frankfurt: Peter Lang, 2007), 259.

21. "El primer sentimiento de Hladík fue de mero terror. Pensó que no lo hubieran arredrado la horca, la decapitación o el degüello, pero que morir fusilado era intolerable. En vano se redijo que el acto puro y general de morir era lo temible, no las circunstancias concretas. No se cansaba de imaginar esas circunstancias: absurdamente procuraba agotar todas las variaciones. Anticipaba infinitamente el proceso, desde el insomne amanecer hasta la misteriosa descarga." Borges, *Obras Completas*, 1:509; Borges, *Labyrinths*, 89.

22. Jerusalem finally commits suicide in the face of Zur Linde's torture.

23. "Se cierne ahora sobre el mundo una época implacable. Nosotros la forjamos, nosotros que ya somos su víctima. ¿Qué importa que Inglaterra sea el martillo y nosotros el yunque? Lo importante es que rija la violencia, no las serviles timideces cristianas. Si la victoria y la injusticia y la felicidad no son para Alemania, que sean para otras naciones. Que el cielo exista, aunque nuestro lugar sea el infierno." Borges, *Obras Completas*, 1:581; Borges, *Labyrinths*, 147.

24. Hannah Arendt, *Eichmann in Jerusalem* (New York: Viking, 1965), 22.

25. "Miro mi cara en el espejo para saber quién soy, para saber cómo me portaré dentro de unas horas, cuando me enfrente con el fin. Mi carne puede tener miedo; yo no." Borges, *Obras Completas*, 1:581; Borges, *Labyrinths*, 147.

26. "Hitler creyó luchar por un país, pero luchó por todos, aun por aquellos que agredió y detestó. No importa que su Yo lo ignorara; lo sabían su sangre, su voluntad." Borges, *Obras Completas*, 1:580.

27. "El mundo se moría de judaísmo y de esa enfermedad del judaísmo, que es la fe de Jesús; nosotros le enseñamos la violencia y la fe de la espada. Esa espada nos mata y somos comparables al hechicero que teje un laberinto y que se ve forzado a errar en él hasta el fin de sus días o a David que juzga a un desconocido y lo condena a muerte y oye después la revelación: 'Tú eres aquel hombre.'" Borges, *Obras Completas*, 1:580.

28. "Muchas cosas hay que destruir para edificar el nuevo orden; ahora sabemos que Alemania era una de esas cosas. Hemos dado algo más que nuestra vida, hemos dado la suerte de nuestro querido país. Que otros maldigan y otros lloren; a mí me regocija que nuestro don sea orbicular y perfecto." Borges, *Obras Completas*, 1:580.

29. Dominick LaCapra, *Representing the Holocaust: History, Theory, Trauma* (Ithaca, NY: Cornell University Press, 1994), 169–203.

30. "Si yo tuviera el trágico honor de ser alemán, no me resignaría a sacrificar a la mera eficacia militar la inteligencia y la probidad de mi patria. . . . Es posible que una derrota alemana sea la ruina de Alemania; es indiscutible que su victoria sería la ruina y el envilecimiento del orbe." Jorge Luis Borges, "Ensayo de imparcialidad," *Sur* 61 (October 1939): 29. In this essay, Borges equated a Nazi victory in Europe with the hypothetical seizure of power by Argentine fascism: "No me refiero al imaginario peligro de una aventura colonial sudamericana; pienso en los imitadores autóctonos, en los *Uebermenschen* caseros que el inexorable azar nos depararía."

31. "Un rostro condenado a ser una mascara . . . un hombre lapidado, incendiado y ahogado en cámaras letales." Borges, "Israel," in *Obras Completas*, 2:375.

32. Jacques Lacan, *The Four Fundamental Concepts of Psycho-Analysis* (New York: Norton, 1981), 55–56, 68–70, 121–131, 275.

33. On the fascist unconscious and psychoanalytic theory, see Federico Finchelstein, *A Brief History of Fascist Lies* (Oakland: University of California Press, 2020), 58–74.

34. "En el argumento que he bosquejado intuía la invención más apta para disimular sus defectos y para ejercitar sus felicidades, la posibilidad de rescatar (de manera simbólica) lo fundamental de su vida." Borges, *Obras Completas*, 1:510; Borges, *Labyrinths*, 91.

35. "Dio término a su drama: no le faltaba ya resolver sino un solo epíteto. Lo encontró; la gota de agua resbaló en su mejilla. Inició un grito enloquecido, movió la cara, la cuádruple descarga lo derribó. Jaromir Hladík murió el veintinueve de marzo, a las nueve y dos minutos de la mañana." Borges, *Obras Completas*, 1:512–513; Borges, *Labyrinths*, 94.

36. On the *Musselman*, see Primo Levi, *The Drowned and the Saved* (New York: Vintage, 1989). On the concept of empathic unsettlement, see Dominick LaCapra, *Writing History, Writing Trauma* (Baltimore: Johns Hopkins University Press, 2000), 78.

37. This is the case of detective Erik Lönnroth, the rational, and eventually misguided, investigator of the symbolic. Lönnroth follows the conceptual traces that, according to his interpretation, were left behind by the killers in the assassination of the kabbalist Marcelo Yarmolinsky. He ends up assassinated in the story and we learn that the explanation for both crimes is not symbolic and conceptually sophisticated, but rather explicitly selfish and grounded in ordinary human actions. Yarmolinsky was not killed for symbolic reasons. He is robbed and killed by the same perpetrators who, in an act of revenge, also kill Lönnroth.

38. Borges, *Obras Completas*, 1:579; Borges, *Labyrinths*, 145.

39. Elie Wiesel, *Night* (New York: Bantam, 1982), 109.

5. A Fascist History

1. Carl Schmitt, *Glossarium* (Milan: Giuffrè, 2001), entry 30-9-50, 434.

2. Reflecting on the relevance of Carl Schmitt's work for the historiography of violence, Benjamin Brower cogently argued that "Schmitt can serve historians of war and violence seeking finely tuned perspectives to reveal the complex configurations of violence that might elude explanations based on 'straight' or reconstructive readings of archives." See Benjamin Brower, "Partisans and Populations: The Place of Civilians in War, Algeria (1954–62)," *History and Theory* 56, no. 3 (2017): 397.

3. As Matthew Specter writes with respect to Schmitt's conception of Grossraum,

> Schmitt's own investment in the quasi-mythical figures of land and sea that are his inheritance from Atlantic geopolitical tradition reveals his entrapment in fundamentalist ontologies of power and commitment to a certain logic of historical development. His equivocation on the question of whether the Soviet Union was a

Grossraum—was it a fellow land power deserving of respect, or the embodiment of a decadent universalism?—exemplifies the tensions that erupt when the ontological features of the theory collide with the contingencies of singular events, in this case the Third Reich's changing decisions about friend and foe.

Grossraum cannot be at once the master key to the past rise and fall of empires, a necessary structural principle of future world order, and consistent with a robust account of human agency in history.

See Matthew Specter, "Grossraum and Geopolitics: Resituating Schmitt in an Atlantic Context," *History and Theory* 56, no. 3 (2017): 406.

4. Reinhart Koselleck, *The Practice of Conceptual History* (Stanford: Stanford University Press, 2002), 119.

5. See the insightful reading of Koselleck in María Pía Lara, *The Disclosure of Politics: Struggles Over the Semantics of Secularization* (New York: Columbia University Press, 2013), 125–140.

6. See Martin Jay, *Reason After Its Eclipse: On Late Critical Theory* (Madison: University of Wisconsin Press, 2016), 36, 37, 183.

7. Carl Schmitt, "La teoría política del mito," in *Carl Schmitt, teólogo de la política*, ed. Héctor Orestes Aguilar (Mexico: Fondo de Cultura Económica 2001), 67.

8. Carl Schmitt, *Hamlet o Hecuba: la irrupción del tiempo en el drama* (Valencia: Pre-Textos, 1994), 39.

9. See Reinhard Mehring, *Carl Schmitt: A Biography* (Cambridge: Polity, 2014), 444.

10. An earlier exponent of this view of Schmitt was Jacob Taubes. He was then followed by other experts such as Heinrich Meier, Roberto Esposito, and Carlo Galli, who also tended to present the *Katechon* as the notion that tied Schmitt's theory of history together. See Jacob Taubes, To *Carl Schmitt: Letters and Reflections* (New York: Columbia University Press, 2013), 12–15. See also Heinrich Meier, *The Lesson of Carl Schmitt: Four Chapters on the Distinction Between Political Theology and Political Philosophy* (Chicago: University of Chicago Press, 1998); Carlo Galli, *La mirada de Jano: ensayos sobre Carl Schmitt* (Buenos Aires: Fondo de Cultura Económica, 2011); Roberto Esposito, *Two: The Machine of Political Theology and the Place of Thought* (New York: Fordham University Press, 2015), 76–82.

11. Mehring, *Carl Schmitt*, 247, 395.

12. Carl Schmitt, *The Nomos of the Earth in the International Law of the Jus Publicum Europaeum* (New York: Telos, 2003), 59–60. See also Schmitt's

rather vague take on the *Katechon* in Carl Schmitt, *Imperium* (Macerata: Quodlibet, 2015). On the notion of the *Katechon*, see Giorgio Agamben, *The Time That Remains: A Commentary on the Letter to the Romans* (Stanford: Stanford University Press, 2005), 108–111; and Massimo Cacciari, *Il potere che frena* (Milan: Adelphi, 2013).

13. Meier, *The Lesson of Carl Schmitt*, 162, Mehring, *Carl Schmitt*, 426–427, 442–443; Schmitt, *Glossarium*, entry of 19-12-47, 91.

14. See Carl Schmitt, "El fuhrer defiende el derecho" (1934), in Aguilar, *Carl Schmitt, teólogo de la política*, 114–118.

15. Alfred Rosenberg, *The Myth of the Twentieth Century* (Torrance, CA: Noontide, 1982).

16. The fascists of *Critica Fascista* enthusiastically agreed with Berdiaeff on the performativity of fascism vis-à-vis the law but disagreed with his statement about the medieval nature of fascism. See "*Fascismo... Medio Evo?*," *Critica Fascista* (April 15, 1927). See Nicolas Berdiaeff, *Una nueva edad media: reflexiones acerca de los destinos de Rusia y Europa* (Barcelona: Apolo, 1933).

17. For Franco, see, for example, Ernesto Gimenez Caballero, "Il Vero volto di Franco," *Gerarchia* (October 1937): 677. For Uriburu and the sacred, see Finchelstein, *Fascismo, liturgia e imaginario: el mito del general Uriburu y la Argentina nacionalista* (Buenos Aires: Fondo de Cultura Económica, 2002), 41–51.

18. "Il fascismo e la sola forza capace di salvare l'Italia, di governarla, dopo averla salvata. Esso sa questo, e la sua forza si trasforma in diritto dinanzi alla sua coscienza. Il Mondo si rende conto di questo, e la forza fascista diventa diritto dinanzi al mondo." Enrico Corradini, "La forza dominante," *Gerarchia* (March 1926): 142–143. On the natural state of the "fascist unitary and organic conception of the state," see Giovanni Selvi, "Le basi natural della dottrina fascista," *Gerarchia* (April 1926): 240.

19. With Hobbesian undertones, Lugones asserted that "Life itself is a state of force. And since 1914 we owe again to the sword this virile confrontation with reality." If reality did not conform to the myth of the leader, it was reality that had to be changed and it was changed by war. Lugones presented the legitimate reasons for a coup when he asserted: "In the conflict of authority with the law, which is more and more frequent because it is an outcome, the man with the sword has to be with authority." Leopoldo Lugones, "La hora de la espada," in *La patria fuerte* (Buenos Aires: Circulo Militar-Biblioteca del Oficial, 1930), 13–19.

20. Leopoldo Lugones, 13–19.

21. "L'uomo economico non esiste, esiste l'uomo integrale, che è politico, che è economico, che è religioso, che è santo, che è guerriero." Benito Mussolini, *Opera Omnia* (Florence: La Fenice, 1951–1962), 26:95.

22. Meier, *The Lesson of Carl Schmitt*, 162.

23. Carl Schmitt, *The Leviathan in the State Theory of Thomas Hobbes* (Chicago: University of Chicago Press, 2008), 82–86.

24. Carl Schmitt, *The Crisis of Parliamentary Democracy* (Cambridge, MA: MIT Press, 1985).

25. Carl Schmitt, *Dictatorship* (Cambridge: Polity, 2015), xxxv; Carl Schmitt, "El ser y el devenir del Estado Fascista" (1929), in Aguilar, *Carl Schmitt, teólogo de la política*, 75–81.

26. Carl Schmitt, *Tierra y mar* (Madrid: Trotta, 2007), 21, 22. See also Carl Schmitt, "*La tensión planetaria* entre Oriente y Occidente y la oposición de Tierra y Mar," *Revista de Estudios Políticos* 81 (1955): 4.

27. Chiara Bottici, *Philosophy of Political Myth* (Cambridge: Cambridge University Press, 2007), 230, 231; and Andreas Kalyvas, *Democracy and the Politics of the Extraordinary: Max Weber, Carl Schmitt and Hannah Arendt* (Cambridge: Cambridge University Press, 2008), 121.

28. Georges Sorel, *Reflections on Violence* (New York: Peter Smith, 1941), 135.

29. See Andreas Kalyvas's criticism of Habermas's reading of Schmitt in his *Democracy and the Politics of the Extraordinary*, 120. See also Jan-Werner Müller, *A Dangerous Mind: Carl Schmitt in Post-War European Thought* (New Haven, CT: Yale University Press, 2003), 28. For a contrasting reading on Habermas and Schmitt, see Matthew Specter, *Habermas: An Intellectual Biography* (Cambridge: Cambridge University Press, 2010), 11–12, 17, 211.

30. Hannah Arendt, *The Origins of Totalitarianism* (New York: Meridian, 1959), 339. On Schmitt's theology, Catholicism, and anti-Judaism, see Carlo Ginzburg, *Nondimanco* (Milan: Adelphi, 2018), 13.

31. Schmitt, *The Crisis of Parliamentary Democracy*, 75, 76. See Ernesto Laclau, *On Populist Reason* (London: Verso, 2005); Andrew Arato, "Political Theology and Populism," in *The Promise and Perils of Populism: Global Perspectives*, ed. Carlos de la Torre (Lexington: University Press of Kentucky, 2015). See also my analysis of Laclau in *From Fascism to Populism in History* (Oakland: University of California Press, 2017), 94–95, 140–142, 147, 212–215.

32. Mehring, *Carl Schmitt*, 339; and Wolfgang Schieder, *Mythos Mussolini: Deutsche in Audienz beim Duce* (Munich: Oldenbourg Wissenschaftsverlag, 2013), 315–316.

33. "Noi abbiamo creato il nostro mito. Il mito è una fede, è una passione. Non è necessario che sia una realtà. È una realtà nel fatto che è un pungolo, che

è una speranza, che è fede, che è coraggio. Il nostro mito è la Nazione, il nostro mito è la grandezza della Nazione! E a questo mito, a questa grandezza, che noi vogliamo tradurre in una realtà completa, noi subordiniamo tutto il resto." Benito Mussolini, "Il discorso di Napoli," in *Opera Omnia* (Florence: La Fenice, 1951–1962), 38:457. See also Schmitt, *The Crisis of Parliamentary Democracy*, 75, 76.

34. See Carl Schmitt, *Political Romanticism* (New Brunswick, NJ: Transaction, 2011), 160.

35. See Helmut Quaritsch, ed., *Carl Schmitt-Antworten in Nürnberg* (Berlin: Duncker und Humblot, 2000); see the English translations in *Telos* 72 (1987): 91–129; and *Telos*, 139 (2007): 35–43.

36. Schmitt, *Glossarium*, entry 13-9-50.

37. Carl Schmitt, *Ex Captivitate Salus*, ed. Andreas Kalyvas and Federico Finchelstein (Cambridge: Polity, 2017), 87.

38. Schmitt, 71.

39. See Andreas Kalyvas and Federico Finchelstein, editors' introduction to Carl Schmitt, *Ex Captivitate Salus*, 6–7.

40. Carl Schmitt, "Historiographia in Nuce: Alexis de Tocqueville," *Revista de estudios políticos* 43 (1949): 109–116; and also in Schmitt, *Ex Captivitate Salus*, 25–31.

41. Kalyvas and Finchelstein, editors' introduction to Carl Schmitt, *Dialogues on Power and Space*, 7.

42. Koselleck, *The Practice of Conceptual History*, 55, 119.

43. See Carl Schmitt, "*Hamlet y Jacobo I de Inglaterra*," *Revista de Estudios Políticos* 85 (1956): 86; and Schmitt, *Hamlet o Hecuba*, 38, 45.

44. Enzo Traverso, *Fire and Blood: The European Civil War* (New York: Verso, 2016).

Conclusion

1. Ernst Cassirer, *The Myth of the State* (New York: Doubleday, 1955 [1946]), 373.

2. "Un creador de mitos," afirmaba que, "si toda palabra es en el fondo una imagen, toda frase es en el fondo un mito completo."

3. Leopoldo Lugones, *El Payador* (Buenos Aires: Otero Impresores, 1916), 6; and Leopoldo Lugones, *Escritos políticos* (Buenos Aires: Losada, 2009), 334–337.

4. Borges, *Leopoldo Lugones* (Buenos Aires: Troquel, 1955), 60.

5. Lugones prometeo. See also Graciela Ferràs, "Filosofía, mito y nación en el Prometeo de Leopoldo Lugones," *Cuyo: Anuario de Filosofía Argentina y Americana* 24 (2007).

6. Plínio Salgado, *Palavra Nova dos Tempos Novos*, in *Obras Completas* (São Paulo: Editôra das Américas, 1954–1956), 7:279. On Brazillian fascism, see Hélgio Trindade, *Integralismo: o fascismo brasileiro na década de 30* (São Paulo: Difel, 1979); Sandra McGee Deutsch, *Las Derechas: The Extreme Right in Argentina, Brazil, and Chile, 1890–1939* (Stanford: Stanford University Press, 1999); Leandro Pereira Gonçalves and Odilon Caldeira Neto, *O fascismo em camisas verdes: do integralismo ao neointegralismo* (Rio de Janeiro: FGV Editora, 2020).

7. Mike Cronin, "The Blueshirt Movement, 1932–5: Ireland's Fascists?," *Journal of Contemporary History* 30, no. 2 (April 1995): 315.

8. Lloyd E. Eastman, "Fascism in Kuomintang China: The Blue Shirts," *China Quarterly* 49 (January-March 1972): 9. On fascism in China, see also Maggie Clinton, *Revolutionary Nativism: Fascism and Culture, 1925–1937* (Durham, NC: Duke University Press, 2017); Brian Tsui, *China's Conservative Revolution: The Quest for a New Order, 1927–1949* (Cambridge: Cambridge University Press, 2018).

9. Federico Finchelstein, *From Fascism to Populism in History* (Oakland: University of California Press, 2017), 78.

10. See Carl Schmitt, *Glossarium* (Seville: El paseo, 2021), 268, 326. See also Camillo Pellizzi, "Concetto del regime fascista," *Critica Fascista* (January 15, 1926): 28. It was this conversion of unconscious drives into their conscious political incarnation that made the fascists fanatical of seekers of inner authenticity. Their leader led the search. As Enrico Corradini argued, Mussolini's leadership combined "a profound instinct and high consciousness." His followers were seekers of the truth without rational mediations. Enrico Corradini, "Dopo le opere compiute," *Il Giornale d'Italia*, March 12, 1929. See a similar argument in Giorgio Pini, "Divagazioni," *Critica Fascista* (February 1, 1928): 51.

11. "Yo comprendo que las juventudes italianas tengan de su Duce una reverencia mítica, religiosa. Porque conocen su vida. Y han contemplado su mirar que les dice de un golpe más secretos aún que su vida misma." See Ernesto Giménez Caballero, *Genio de España: Exaltaciones a una resurrección nacional y del mundo* (Zaragoza: Ediciones Jerarquía, 1938), 160; and also Caballero, "Mussolini predestinato dal popolo e della storia," *Universalità fascista* (July-August, 1932): 378.

12. See Sergio Panunzio, "Idee sul fascismo," *Critica Fascista* (March 15, 1925): 105. See also Valentino Piccoli, "Il pensiero político di Mussolini," *Meridiani* 11–12 (1936): 10; Vicenzo Morello, "I vecchi partiti e il fascismo," *Gerarchia* (March 1923): 822, 807.

13. "Il vero uomo d'azione che ha senso pratico sul serio è anche sempre un teorico sebbene di una sua speciale manera . . . che ha l'attitudine a conquistarsi e riconquistarsi continuamente le sue verità per un sforzo rapido d'intuito." See Balbino Giuliano, "Le ragioni storiche del fascismo," *Gerarchia* (June 1925): 379.

14. Libero Merlino, "Il Fascismo come dottrina," *Gerarchia* (July 1927): 530–531.

15. Merlino argued that "Il fascism, novello Prometeo, ha rapito a quell'Olimpo la scintilla che l'aveva illuminato un tempo ma che ora stave per spegnersi-lo spirito rinnovatore, il fremito rivoluzionario." Merlino, 531–536. See also Volt, *Gerarchia* (February 1924): 110.

16. For instance, by referring to the self and criticizing the abstract approach of Benedetto Croce and liberalism, Pellizzi attempted to recuperate what was insinuated in "old" theories. He argued: "Ma nel suo centro è ancora il punto vitale, il dèmone instabile, maligno, rivoluzionatore: Io, il soggetto, il soggetto totale della realtà, che è vivo, sebbene la realtà (di lui stesso) sia." See Camillo Pellizzi, "Croce: L'ultimo della borghesia," *Gerarchia* (November 1923): 1360.

17. See the discussion in Finchelstein, *A Brief History of Fascist Lies* (Oakland: University of California Press, 2020).

18. Jorge Luis Borges, "Ragnarök," in *El Hacedor* (Buenos Aires: Emecé Editores, 1992), 46–47.

19. Borges, 47.

20. José Carlos Mariátegui, *La escena contemporánea* (Lima: Minerva, 1925), 122. For key approaches to Mariátegui, see the works of José Sazbón and Juan De Castro. See by José Sazbón, *Historia y representación* (Buenos Aires: Universidad Nacional de Quilmes, 2002) 114–155 and *Nietzsche en Francia y otros estudios de historia intelectual* (Buenos Aires: Universidad Nacional de Quilmes, 2009), 417–427; and Juan De Castro, *Bread and Beauty: The Cultural Politics of José Carlos Mariátegui* (Chicago: Haymarket, 2021).

21. For a paradigmatic example of this functionalist historiography on myth, see Ian Kershaw, *The Hitler Myth* (New York: Oxford University Press, 1987).

Index

INDEX

Levi, Primo, 63, 66,
Liberalism, 7, 9, 40, 42, 68, 70, 71, 81,
102, 106, 108
Louis, Annick, 147
Lombroso, Cesare, 141
Lugones, Leopoldo, ix, 11, 28, 29, 101,
113, 114
Lukacs, Georg, 131

Malaparte, Curzio, 11
Mariátegui, José Carlos, x, 5, 26, 96,
103, 122
Marxism, Marxist, 26, 102, 103, 122
Mehring Reinhard, 98
Meier Heinrich, 102, 159
Meinvielle, Julio Fr., 35, 68
Merlino Libero, 117
Mexico, 152
Mezzasoma, Fernando, 41
Mosse, George, 129
Mussolini, Benito, vii, ix, x, 9, 10, 11,
13, 15, 27, 28, 30,31, 32, 33, 35, 36,
37, 41, 43, 44, 45, 47, 48, 49, 50,
51, 52, 53, 55, 56, 57, 58, 59, 70, 72,
101, 102, 103, 105, 106, 107, 108, 116,
122, 150

nación, La, 70
Nationalism, nationalist,
nacionalismo, 7, 29, 41, 42, 44, 70,
81, 84, 86, 105; as "liberal jihad,"
22, 70
Nazi, Nazism, viii, 1, 2, 19, 23, 24,
25, 33, 37, 38, 44, 46, 52, 53, 54,
55, 61, 62, 64, 65, 69, 70, 73, 74,
75, 76, 78, 79, 80, 81, 82, 84, 86,
88, 89, 90, 91, 98, 99, 102, 105,
106, 107; *führerprinzip,* 89;
National Socialism, 105,
party, 75

Nietzsche, Friedrich, 51, 61, 74;
Nietzschean, 62, 75

Orientalism, orientalist, 56, 57

Palacio, Ernesto, 156
Panunzio, Sergio, 117
Pastormelo, Sergio, 146
Pellizzi, Camillo, 42
Peronism, 60; anti-Peronism, 120
popular sovereignty, ix
populism, populist, 64, 69
Prometheus, myth of, 8, 14, 16, 28,
37, 43, 44, 47, 50, 51, 53, 56, 57, 58,
59, 113, 114, 117, 118
Psychoanalysis, 4, 5, 11, 12, 16, 17, 18,
23, 26, 27, 28, 29, 30, 33, 34, 35, 36,
38, 45, 46, 47, 48, 54, 60

racism, racist, 15, 18, 21, 22, 38, 73, 123
Ramos Mejía, José María, 154
Rancière, Jacques, 141
Rocco Alfredo, 41, 71
Rosas, Juan Manuel de, 67, 68, 141
Rose, Gillian, 143
Rosenberg, Alfred, 99, 100
Russell, Bertrand, 74
Russia, 10

Salgado, Plinio, x, 11, 114, 115
San Martin, José de, 153
Sarfatti, Marguerita, 72
Sarlo, Beatriz, 68, 73
Sarmiento, Domingo Faustino, 66,
68, 149
Sazbón, José, 164
Schmitt, Carl, x, xi, 9, 10, 18, 19, 94,
95, 97, 98, 99, 100, 101, 102, 103,
104, 105, 106, 107, 108, 109, 110,
111, 112, 116; *The Crisis of*

NEW DIRECTIONS IN CRITICAL THEORY
Amy Allen, General Editor

GPSR Authorized Representative: Easy Access System Europe, Mustamäe tee
50, 10621 Tallinn, Estonia, gpsr.requests@easproject.com